Visita nos

American University Studies

Series VII
Theology and Religion

Vol. 203

PETER LANG
New York • Washington, D.C./Baltimore • Boston
Bern • Frankfurt am Main • Berlin • Vienna • Paris

Thomas S. Ferguson

Visita nos

Reception, Rhetoric, and Prayer in a North African Monastery

PETER LANG
New York • Washington, D.C./Baltimore • Boston
Bern • Frankfurt am Main • Berlin • Vienna • Paris

Library of Congress Cataloging-in-Publication Data

Ferguson, Thomas S.
Visita nos: reception, rhetoric, and prayer in
a North African monastery / Thomas S. Ferguson.
p. cm. — (American university studies. VII, Theology and religion; vol. 203)
Includes bibliographical references and index.
1. Catholic Church. Psalter collects (Visita nos). 2. Fulgentius, Saint, Bishop
of Ruspa, 468–533. 3. Psalter collects—History and criticism. 4. Rhetoric,
Ancient. I. Title. II. Series: American university studies.
Series VII, Theology and religion; vol. 203.
BX2015.7.A24F47   264'.15—dc21   97-29513
ISBN 0-8204-3911-8
ISSN 0740-0446

Die Deutsche Bibliothek-CIP-Einheitsaufnahme

Ferguson, Thomas S.:
Visita nos: reception, rhetoric, and prayer in
a North African monastery / Thomas S. Ferguson.
–New York; Washington, D.C./Baltimore; Boston; Bern;
Frankfurt am Main; Berlin; Vienna; Paris: Lang.
(American university studies: Ser. 7, Theology and religion; Vol. 203)
ISBN 0-8204-3911-8

The paper in this book meets the guidelines for permanence and durability
of the Committee on Production Guidelines for Book Longevity
of the Council of Library Resources.

Printed in the United States of America

For

Dan, Maureen, Bethany & Erica

CONTENTS

ABBREVIATIONS

ACW   *Ancient Christian Writers*

AJP   *The American Journal of Philology*

CC   *Corpus Christianorum. Series latina*

CSEL   *Corpus scriptorum ecclesiasticorum latinorum*

DTC   *Dictionaire de Théologie Catholique*

JBC   *The Jerome Biblical Commentary*

JEH   *The Journal of Ecclesiastical History*

JES   *The Journal of Ecumenical Studies*

JRS   *The Journal of Roman Studies*

JSS   *The Journal of Semitic Studies*

JTS   *The Journal of Theological Studies*

PG   *Patrologia Graeca* (ed. Migne)

PL   *Patrologia Latina* (ed. Migne)

RB   *Regula Benedicta*

SP   *Studia Patristica*

SS   *Spicilegium Solesmense* (ed. Pitra)

VC   *Vigilae Christianae*

ZAW   *Zeitschrift für altestamentliche Wissenschaft*

PREFACE

In the early sixth century, in a Catholic monastery in the Vandal kingdom of North Africa, an abbot composed an exegesis on the Book of Psalms within the context of their use in the Divine Office. In order to enhance the daily prayer of his monks, he focused their meditation on particular themes on the psalms. He identified and highlighted selected verses with the dual aims of teaching Christian theology and offering temporal support to a beleaguered community.

He chose to achieve his aim during the brief pause between psalms in the daily Office. Eastern monastic tradition provided him with a liturgical from particularly suited to his needs, the psalm collect. By carefully exploiting the arrangement of psalms, he was able to meet the need for theological orthodoxy and liturgical conciseness, and to carry on the sort of theological warfare in which the African Church was adept. Besides addressing the presence of the Arian Vandals, the orations dealt with the Donatists, countering Pelagians theology, and teaching Chalcedonian orthodoxy.

The abbot was able to compose brief orations for exegetical tasks because of the shift of emphasis in rhetorical practice. Classical rhetoric had long since been put to less exalted usages. The advent of Christianity, and the resultant loss of classical education for the masses was not the cause, but rather the beneficiary of this shift. As Gibbon laments, by the second century C. E., "(although) the authority of Plato and Aristotle, of Zeno and Epicurus, still reigned in the schools and their systems, transmitted with blind deference from one generation of disciples to another, precluded every generous attempt to exercise the powers or enlarge the limits of the human mind." He further states that, "the name...of Orator had been usurped by the sophists."

Gibbon hits upon the factor that enervated classical rhetoric, lack of purpose. Christian appropriation of rhetoric had an abundant sense of purpose and design. That it's rhetorical forms so fitfully corresponded with those of classical expression made the transmission of the Christian message that much more effective.As the world received and digested this message, rhetoric took on new forms to conform to the new message.

This study evaluates the rhetorical usefulness of liturgical expression through the collects of this African monk, whom I have identified as Fulgentius of Ruspe. After a brief survey of the shift from classical to Christian rhetoric, the study will continue with a literary, historical and theological examination of the collects and their approach to the Church as a whole and to the specific needs of a monastic community living under siege.

An important tool in investigating Fulgentius' rhetoric is offered by modern literary criticism, especially Reception Theory.Fulgentius was author of the collects and interpreter ofthe psalms, who chose specific verses for interpretation in a limited literary form.Chapter 4 of this study highlights some of his choices, placing them into the context of modern genre studies and his historical milieu.

Among the people who have helped with the preparation of this book, first and foremost my thanks goes to Rev. Joseph T. Lienhard, S.J., of Fordham University, without whose collaboration the collect translations could not have been as accurate as I feel they are (although I take full responsibility for any errors). Additional thanks goe to Dr. Harry Nasuti of Fordham University, who introduced me to modern literary and genre theory. Professor John Keber, of Manhattan College, who read the manuscript and offered many helpful comments. Louis Hamilton of Fordham University proofread the manuscript and also offered suggestions on presentation. Nancy Cave of Manhattan College gave assistance with word processing questions.

Scriptural quotations are translated from the Vulgate, and the psalms are numbered according to the Septuagint.

INTRODUCTION

Rhetoric in the Christian Liturgy

Rhetoric and the Scriptures

During the early period of Christian reception of the Scriptures, the resistance of classically educated persons to their lack of classical structures eventually gave way to an acceptance of a message presented within a rhetorically unusual form. Readers of the Scriptures perceived signs of persuasive language, but the mode of persuasion was the miraculous event rather than the logical argument. All persuasive speech emerges from the inspiration of the Holy Spirit rather than from oratorical training.[1] Redaction of the biblical texts for theological and political purposes further obscured the original structure of prophetic utterances. Add to this a lack of a tradition for analysis of expression, and, to a potential Christian convert with a Hellenistic background, the Scriptures lacked rhetorical content.

Prophetic discourse directed a divine message towards an audience of people who lived in a covenantal relationship with God, and who therefore approached the divine with the mien of suppliant partners rather than with the reason of a judicial body or those engaged in debate. Prophets deal with the past, present and future of the covenant, and reminded Israel of its responsibilities. The dialectic is limited, but not totally one-sided, though Israel's role tended towards observance and dedication rather than verbal discourse. Words are the counsel of the "senior partner," to be followed, if necessary, by miraculous acts.[2]

As for the Christian Scriptures, some of Paul's discourses in the Acts of the Apostles offered some recognizable rhetorical content for educated Christians,[3] but the utterances of Jesus did not. Even the Sermon on the Mount,[4] a central, although reconstructed, discourse, provided no oratorical link to classical rhetoric.

Whether or not rhetoric was in the mind of the writers of the Hebrew Bible, Christians perceived some rhetorical form, though still not in the classical analytical mode, in biblical poetry, wisdom literature, and allegory. Later Christian exegesis employed allegory, and Christian interpretation began to draw out the rhetoric of psalm texts through the liturgical constructs of doxology, antiphon, and collect.

Classical Rhetoric and the Christian Message

The rhetorical world in which the Scriptures were disseminated was Roman. Roman oratory, as lamented by Gibbon,[5] was devoid of purpose due to the separation of rhetoric from philosophy, and the devolution of prose style to the needs of bureaucracies and commerce. Yet, early Christians needed to appease the Roman world in order to end or curb persecutions, and Greek Christian orators made a necessary connection: by linking hellenistic cultural heritage to the positive, practical goal of Christian apologetics and proselytization, Christians could deal with the Roman world in terms that it could accept.[6] This linking of new thought to traditional style did not immediately achieve its practical goal, that of ending persecution, but it gave to Christianity an extra-scriptural mode of expression, one with which educated Christians were comfortable.[7]

Liturgical Rhetoric

As Christianity could not secure for itself a place in the world of public discourse in order to preach its message, some other venue of effective communication was needed. Uneducated people, who as a matter of course would pick up all the theology they needed to know concerning Roman religion during their daily lives, could not assimilate Christian doctrine as readily through the cultic aspects of the weekly liturgical meeting available to them. In order to deal with a complex theology, homiletics and liturgical constructs developed within the cult to serve as teaching tools for the faithful.

Early Church leaders needed a vast array of rhetorical skills in order to fulfill their roles as speakers, teachers, controversialists, letter and treatise writers, and preachers. The role of priest developed from the cultic functionary of Roman religion to that of educated leader. Priestly education centered upon Scripture rather than the classical disciplines, yet they practiced the persuasive art in their own manner.[8] Oratory in the form of homiletics allowed preachers to systematize doctrine for the people. Within the context of a liturgical service, the faithful heard wisdom from the Scriptures and exegetical comments on that wisdom from their preacher. Illiterate Christians, therefore, were as able to assimilate doctrine as well as the literate.

Even more effective aids to teaching appeared in the form of liturgical structures, concise, prayerful, public utterances which taught orthodox theology while they addressed God. The necessity of employing prayer as a teaching tool developed as a response to heterodoxy which appeared all-too-soon in the history of Christianity.[9] As psalms were the liturgical texts which were in widest use among Christians,[10] they had great value as teaching tools. The need for the appropriation of all scriptural texts into a Christian context led to collections of commentaries and sermons, as well as to the liturgical constructs which were placed in proximity to the psalm texts in order to enhance their value for Christian worship.

Christian Psalm Interpretation

Christians were not the first worshipping community to develop a hermeneutical link with the psalms. Psalm titles, which gradually became accepted as part of the scriptural canon, indicated the need among the Israelites to relate the psalms closely to a figure, most often David, or figures from the scriptural narrative.[11] Midrashic texts offered further commentary, but psalm titles provided immediate recourse to those who wished to apply the often difficult poetic imagery to familiar circumstantial references.

Christians made use of this liturgical example. As the revelation of the Hebrew Scriptures, in Greek and Latin translations, became regarded as a "shadow" of the Christian Scriptures, the ubiquity of the psalms in Christian worship needed justification. The more violent images needed reconciling with Christian teachings of forgiveness, and cultic references needed to be seen within a Christian context. As Christian interpretations of prophecy centered on the fullness of the redemptive plan, the psalms provided a key to this plan. David came to be portrayed as a prophetic figure, and the psalms became his prophetic text.[12] The voice of Christ became discernable in the psalms, and the many shadows were illuminated for Christians.

Psalm Interpretation and Liturgical Rhetoric

As psalm interpretation developed among Christians, lengthy commentaries by such luminaries as Origen, Augustine and Cassiodorus served as the primary exegetical texts. Except for Augustine's commentary, which was planned as a series of sermons, the hermeneutical value of commentaries was limited to those Christians who could read and, subsequently, teach them to other educated Christians. Concentrating, as they do, upon theological topics such as christology, piety, ecclesiology, liturgy, or, in recent commentaries, forms and genres, they were works for private or schoolroom study. More available to the worshipping community were those elements of psalm interpretation that appeared in the liturgy as accompaniments to the psalms. As a liturgical meeting proceeds through a fixed time period, interpretative elements: doxology, antiphons, and psalm collects, appear and are passed on in the context of a larger whole. Yet, in the process of singing the Divine Office, the additions to the psalms had an impact on Christian faith that commentaries and homilies were not able to offer.

In spite of their brevity, the additions to the psalms performed the considerable task of Christianizing them, normalizing their theology for the faithful. By placing liturgical structures around a psalm, Christians could receive the entirety of the text's revelation, guided by the structures towards those specific textual elements which best mirrored Christian thought. Through the use of liturgical hermeneutic forms, the Church made value judgments even as it accepted the entire psalter, distancing itself from its uncomfortable elements without appearing to reject any portion of inspired writings. Liturgical structures enabled the faithful to incorporate Christian theology into their lives on an intimate basis in the same manner that the Greco-Roman cults had effected the lives of their followers.

The Doxology

By reciting the doxology (*Gloria patri...*) after each psalm, Christian usage followed the model of the doxologies which appear at the end of each book of the psalter.[13] The doxology's present form[14] was set by the end of the fourth century. Affirming, as they do, the Trinity and its pre-existence, the two portions of the prayer served obvious anti-heretical functions. Its clear defense against Arianism would nominate it for recurring usage in the liturgy of the community of the *Africana* collects. As a rhetorical device, it functioned as a credal statement, a frequent reminder of proper Trinitarian belief, eventually working itself into the consciousness so that one would automatically pray the doxology from memory, as a matter of course after each psalm. Within the briefest of prayers, an entire theology could be affirmed and taught over and over again.

Antiphons

The development of the antiphon texts in Christian liturgy occurred after the time of the *Africana* collects.[15] As a musical practice, however, antiphonal singing, alternating two choirs in the chanting of psalm verses, is mentioned as early as the time of the Chronicler,[16] and among Christians of the first century.[17]

As texts, antiphons were chosen to surround a psalm from either a particular verse from that psalm, or were composed to commemorate a Church season, a saint's memorial, or to highlight a theological teaching. As with the doxology, the use of antiphonal texts was important to the development of liturgical rhetoric in the Church, although it was unknown in sixth-century North Africa.

Psalm Collects

The practice of reciting a collect in connection with psalms developed within the monastic tradition. Pseudo-Athanasius refers to the practice,[18] as does Aetheria's travelogue.[19] John Cassian traces the custom to Egypt, where, after each psalm, the monks would stand, pray silently, prostrate themselves, and then listen to the prayer leader recite a collect.[20] *The Rule of the Master* included the praying of psalm collects, but Benedict, who advocated a simpler prayer life, did not.[21] As the Benedictine observance spread throughout Western Europe, the practice of reciting collects began to decline. By the eighth century, the practice seems to have disappeared altogether.[22]

The three series of psalm collects studied by Dom Louis Brou[23] added to the testimony of the ancient sources, indicate that the practice, though short-lived, had currency in North Africa.

Literary Theory and Psalm Collects

Classically trained Christian writers never quite gave up their literary and philosophical authors and backgrounds, no matter how much they may have excoriated them in their treatises. Rhetoric was too beneficial for expressing and diseminating the Christian message to be rejected as a practice in itself. Even though they are brief in length and curt in expression, psalm collects contain interpretative content pertaining to three areas of classical literary criticism and rhetorical usage: mimesis, reception, and the hermeneutic bridge (catharsis). Whether the author of the *Africana* collects was aware of it or not, his compositions exhibit these critical tools.

Mimesis

Rhetorically, the additions to the psalms, while lacking the developmental intricacies of classical oratory, effectively presented Christian theology to cenobites as well as to the masses of the faithful. They offered a mimetic completion of the psalms, accomplished in the light of Christ's revelation. Mimesis of this sort was initially rejected by Christian writers as being an act of creation, and thus a blasphemous addition to the perfect revelation of Scripture. In effect, any writer practicing mimesis presumed to enter a provenance reserved for divine action.[24]

In spite of this early judgment, mimesis eventually became the accepted mode of composing prayers, imitating, at first, the forms and language of Jewish prayer. The collect form itself appears in truncated versions in the Eighteen Benedictions of the morning prayer service,[25] Once it had been accepted by the Church, the content of the collect form came under the careful control of episcopal decrees. Collect composition, therefore, became less a true mimesis than a theological or pietistic statement composed within a ready-made liturgical form.

Classical Reception

Christian appropriation of classical literary reception is important to the composition of the *Africana* collects. Classical usage of reception allowed an author to both portray, and thus make present to the reader, events of the historical past (either factual or fictional history), and concentrated on the realm of the senses. By late antiquity, Christians had rejected the "lies of the poets" in favor of spiritual representation of the "invisible past" as an eschatological interpretation of salvation history. In scriptural interpretation, the shift of interpretative emphasis from classical to Christian was important because the Latin of the Scriptures remained a foreign mode of rhetorical expression for those Christians who were trained in the classical style.[26]

The Church received the psalms differently from the Synagogue, whose midrashic commentaries on psalm titles and the texts of the psalm themselves had a different exegetical purpose from Christian reception. Whereas, for the Synagogue, the revelation of the psalms was full and complete, for the Church, it was not. Besides the larger theological questions of soteriological importance, local church situations such as saints' cults and theological and pietistic movements called for more specific reception and interpretation of the revelation of the psalms. While the longer exegetical works were the responsibilities of their authors, and came under close and exhaustive scrutiny by the protectors of orthodoxy, liturgical texts received biblical theology in a different manner and needed to follow the guidelines set forth by episcopal synods for approval (see below). A collect was heard by the community of the faithful, who brought it into a particular mind set during the act of worship. Because of their brevity and immediacy, the collects were required to receive Scripture in a mode of pure orthodoxy, or risk tainting the minds of the worshippers with heterodox thought.

The Hermeneutic Bridge

In order to receive such a theologically diverse body of texts as the psalms, the worshipping community needed to place the foreign modes of expression into a personal religious experience. Composition of a mimetic collect frees the listener from literal interpretation of psalm texts, and offers and aesthetic freedom of judgment through which one experiences the "Other" through mimesis. The hermeneutic bridge, or catharsis, was the literary device most easily transferred to Christian rhetorical practice.[27] Augustine wrote of the delights of Christian poetry,[28] and the Medieval concept of *imitatio Christi* was made possible through philosophical hermeneutics. During prayer, the Christian, whether experiencing the weight of sinfulness, siege from spiritual or physical persecution, or a yearning for mystical experience, could connect to the catharsis of feeling through a carefully composed collect which would serve to personalize the psalm.[29]

The daily liturgical praxis of a monastic community did not allow for well-developed sermons at each hour of prayer. The use of psalm collects helped to overcome the limitations of time. They brought living theology to the community, and the need for brevity obliged the author to be clear in his expositions of theological truths. The collect also included the pedagogical advantage of repeating material from the particular psalm which the community had just sung, thus bringing their attention to those passages which the author wished them to address in their personal meditations.

The Fourth-Century Liturgical Reform

A significant amount of new liturgical material appeared in the Western liturgy during the fourth century. Because of the rhetorical power inherent in public prayer, assessment of such material for doctrinal and liturgical orthodoxy needed to occur on a regular basis. In North Africa, where large numbers of texts containing vernacular, barbaric expressions, solecisms and doctrinal errors had begun to appear,[30] synodal decrees attempted to control and direct liturgical activity without suppressing it. Canon 21 of the Synod of Hippo (393) stipulated that all prayers recited at the altar must be addressed to the Father, and that one must avoid using newly composed prayers or prayers composed elsewhere than in the local see until they had been examined by those who knew proper doctrine.[31] The Synod of Carthage (397) took a similar line when faced with prayers suspected of teaching false doctrine.[32] Henceforth, all new liturgical compositions would require official approval.

The *Africana* collects paid scrupulous attention to the requirements of the synods. From his own rhetorical base, the author has taken pains to be doctrinally correct, composing prayers that combine ecclesiastical compatibility with scriptural interpretation and expressive language chosen to give comfort to the oppressed. His texts interpret the psalms on several different levels within the liturgical praxis of the community. Mimetic reception of the psalms enables the author to react to a setting which demands his immediate attention with the creative act.[33] In particular, the anti-Arian and anti-Pelagian passages indicate the interest of the collect author in writing prayers that would both reflect the psalms and offer theologically orthodox lessons to his monks.

A surprising feature of texts composed within such strictures is the immediacy of their concerns. North African synodal tradition would not seem to have approved of such specifically focused prayers, but Vandal persecution offered few opportunities for convening the synod necessary for approval. The existence of these texts indicate that their author had some connection with the local bishop, and possibly composed prayers for an episcopal monastic foundation. The frequent use of *domine* rather than *pater* in address, as required by the synods, reflects the Latin psalter, where *domine* consistently indicates the *prosopon* of the Father rather than that of the Christ.

Sermo Humilis

An important rhetorical device in North African homiletics was *sermo humilis*, the technique of using the Latin language plainly and eschewing the rhetorical flourishes expected by a classically trained congregation. The technique enabled bishops to address their sermons more specifically to those people whose first language was not Latin. The use of *sermo humilis* in the North African liturgy developed out of the theological struggle between the Catholics and the Donatists.[34] The Donatists placed bishops even in the smallest of North African towns, forcing Catholics to do the same. Even so, the two Churches attracted adherents from specific social groups. The Donatists tended towards people whose first language was Berber (Punic), and who occupied the lower rungs on the social ladder, and the Catholics towards those who belonged to the Roman senatorial families who occupied the land well after the fall of Rome's power.[35] Those Berbers whom the Catholics attracted had left the nomadic life for the security of cities and towns, usually farm employees of the senatorial families and residents of the more Romanized (and, thus, less likely to be Donatist) urban centers.

In order to compete with the Donatists who occasionally preached in the Berber language, *sermo humilis* became necessary for Catholic preachers,[36] resulting in a departure from classical rhetoric while keeping the classical language. Preaching in "low" rhetoric without condescension became the hallmark of homilies in late Latin antiquity.[37] More than a form of inverted snobbery, *sermo humilis* enabled bilingual societies in Africa and elsewhere to participate in an exclusively Latin (or Greek) scripture and liturgy.[38] Bishops had the opportunity to practice Christian humility by avoiding fine rhetoric and vocabulary and could be reasonable certain that their preaching would be understood by the members of their congregations.[39]

The simplicity required by *sermo humilis* fit in particularly well with the collects. Their brevity demanded a simple style, and an economy of words that eliminated the possibility for using other rhetorical forms of address. The *Africana* collects take their tone from this homiletic development, and yet, they display a sophisticated understanding of theological and social thought.

CHAPTER 1

The Collect Author

Louis Brou suggested four names as possible authors for the *Africana* collects: Ferrandus, deacon of Carthage, and the bishops Facundus of Hermiane, Verecundus of Junca, and Fulgentius of Ruspe.[1] Brou does not definitively identify the author, but leans towards Verecundus as the most likely candidate, basing his conclusion on the use of words and phrases common to both Verecundus and the collects. However, by adding a thematic investigation to Brou's method, Fulgentius of Ruspe emerges as the more likely of the two to have composed the *Africana* series of psalm collects.

Ferrandus, deacon of Carthage

Ferrandus was a disciple of Fulgentius, whom he accompanied during his exile to Sardinia. He was made a deacon in 520. His works include *Epistolae*,[2] the *Vita Fulgentii*,[3] and a selection of canons from African church councils.[4] According to Facundus of Hermiane, Ferrandus took part in the North African resistance to the condemnation of the Three Chapters.[5]

Epistola 3,[6] written to the Roman deacon Anatolius, affirms the "definition" of Chalcedon concerning the two natures of Christ. In the course of his argumeny, Ferrandus quotes Ps. 84:12: *and to our land he will give his fruit*, proclaiming that the "fruit" is *the seed of David in human substance.*[7] The collect author chooses this verse also, and interprets this:

> *so that your truth, which has been raised up in our land according to the flesh, may give sweetness to those who are consubstantial with him, and bear fruit for you, God and Father.*

Both authors portray christological thought in a manner consonant with Chalcedonian orthodoxy. The language of both writers emerges from their theological assertions rather than from the psalm itself, and both understand the salvific purpose of Christ's humanity. Both authors use Ps. 109:1, *the Lord said to my Lord, sit at my right hand, until I place your enemies as a footstool at your feet*, but offer different interpretations, which are colored by the contexts in which they appear. Ferrandus, in *Epistola* 5,[8] takes the quotation not from the psalter, but from its appearance in Matt. 22:44, its *Sitz im Leben* being an argument between Jesus and the Pharisees. In affirming Jesus Christ's position in the Trinitarian unity, Ferrandus employs Jesus's own use of the verse, which relates King David to the promised Messiah. The Messiah is the son of David, but, that same person (*persona*) is also, as a person of the Trinity, David's Lord. Trinitarian theology enables the believing Christian to give the answer to Jesus's question, "if David thus calls him (the Messiah) Lord, how is he his son?," that the Pharisees could not give.

The collect author interprets the verse in the context of realized eschatology:

> *In the midst of our enemies, Lord, cause us to dominate, so that we who have already merited to sit at your right hand in Christ your son, our creator and Lord, may merit to possess the eternal fatherland with all the saints.*

By using the formula, *Christ, your son*, the collect author indicates an awareness of the psalm verse's appearance in Matthew's Gospel. The further invocation, *our creator and Lord*, offers an anti-Arian interpretation. The opening and closing petitions of the collect are related, as the "enemies," whether they be military, political, or theological, are poised for defeat, with the "fatherland" (political fatherland or heaven) going to the saints, be they the orthodox monks or the saints in heaven.

The similarities of interpretation indicate that both Ferrandus and the collect author were attacking Arian christology, but the collects imply a political solution as well as a theological one. Ferrandus, the monk[9] who became deacon to an urban community, indicates a less worldly interpretation than does the monastery-bound collect author.

Facundus of Hermiane

Facundus (d. after 571), a champion of Chalcedon and defender of the Three Chapters, was imprisoned in a monastery in Constantinople for his dissenting views. His two treatises on the controversy, *Pro defensione trium capitulorum*,[10] addressed to Justinian, and the

Epistola fidei cahtolicae in defensione trium capitulorum,[11] composed while he was in prison, indicate, in their thematic use of the psalms, an affinity with the collects. However, his interpretative aims differ. The collects interpret the psalms in a consistent manner, as befits their liturgical usage, but Facundus uses them as proof texts for particular points in his treatises.

Epistola fidei catholicae quotes Ps. 86:15, *a man was born in her* (i.e., Sion), which the collect renders, *so that in him who as our God on earth was made human.* While both authors use the psalm as a prophecy of Christ's' birth, Facundus employs it as part of his argument that the Incarnate Word is not an absurdity. The collect author, writing well before the condemnation of the Three Chapters, employs the verse as a teaching of Chalcedonian orthodoxy. Facundus used a different psalter from the collect author, indicated by the use of "born" (*natus est*), which appears in several African psalters, including the Psalter of Verona, and the collect author uses "made" (*factus est*), a term which also appears in the Gallican version.

Later on in chapter 2 of the same defense, Facundus interprets Ps. 23:8, *the Lord is strong and mighty; the Lord is mighty in war*, as signifying the power of God against heretics in the person of the pope, evoking Church authority. Collect 23 uses the verse to evoke divine power in heaven, *let Christ, the king of glory, enter them* [i.e., the gates of God's temple] *as if into heaven itself; and now he settles the wars of evil with spiritual (power?).*

Ps. 47:13-14 evokes the city of Sion, *walk around Sion, encompass her; speak in her towers; place your heart in her strength and divide up her houses.* For Facundus, in chapter 12 of his defense, the city signifies the completeness of Church doctrine from which heretics are ejected, while, in Collect 47, *hear what we speak in your towers*, the spiritual city is present within the walls of the monastery itself.

As Brou indicates, there are few similar choices of psalm verses between the collects and Facundus. Moreover, thematic use of those verses eliminates Facundus as the collect author.

Verecundus of Junca

Brou's candidate for collect authorship, Verecundus of Junca was a monk-bishop active from the end of the fifth century to the mid-sixth century.[12] His opposition to the condemnation of the Three Chapters caused him to be called before Justinian to give a statement of faith in 551.   In 552, he retired from episcopal activity to Chalcedon, where he died that same year.[13] Verecundus was a poet and exegete who showed great interest in the documents from the Council of Chalcedon.

Brou's championing of Verecundus as the collect author is based on linguistic, thematic, and stylistic analysis of those portions of Verecundus's great work, *Commentarium super cantica ecclesiastica*[14] that bear closest relationship to the collects. Between commentaries and the collects there are fourteen common psalm verses, which Brou admits could be coincidental, and not enough to positively identify Verecundus as the collect author.[15]

Psalm Verses

Verses with similar interpretations appear in the commentaries on the canticles in Deuteronomy (Deut. 32:1-43) and Daniel (Dan. 3:26-45 - Azaria's canticle).   In the former, both Verecundus and the collect author interpret Ps. 91:5, *as the eagle covers its nest, and over its young, which it loves, expands its wings,* by having the wings refer to the house of God.[16]

Three psalm verses receive similar interpretations in both the commentary on Daniel and the collects. Both authors address Ps. 118:108, *make acceptable the words of my mouth, Lord, and teach me your judgments,* simply, with a view to God's judgment.[17]

Another obvious shared interpretation emerges from Ps. 24:7a, *may you not remember the sins of youth and ignorance, but be mindful of us according to your mercy*, especially as the Daniel excerpt forms a portion of the episode of the Three Young Men in the furnace. The collect author writes for men who have left the activities of their youth behind, and have chosen a life of penitence and atonement.

Finally, both authors connect to the theme of the broken soul and petition God from the position of humility using Ps. 101:4, *my days have vanished like smoke.* Verecundus connects the verse to the assertion in Ps. 50:19 like Ps. 101 a Penitential Psalm, *for a heart contrite and humbled God will not spurn.* The collect expresses confidence that his days and those of his monks will not vanish like smoke due to their mode of living in Christian holiness.

Similar Vocabulary

The phrase *Pharao spiritalis* appears three times in Verecundus's commentary on the Exodus Canticle (Ex. 15:1-18),[18] and in collects 19 and 135. Both authors treat the person of Pharaoh eschatologically:

> *CC* 93,4: *The second glorification, when the Lord suspends the spiritual Pharaoh on the standard of the cross in his passion; the third day, when the same devil, damned with his accomplices standing in the eternal fire.*
> *CC* 93,6: *As that one is an intelligible horse, who by the committing of one sin placed the spiritual Pharaoh upon himself.*
> *CC* 93,15: *When the host of the spiritual Pharaoh receives the capital sentence of ultimate punishment.*
> Collect 19: *Protect us from all evil, so that the spiritual Pharaoh may come to ruin in horses and chariots as we rise up.*
> Collect 135: *When the spiritual Pharaoh has been conquered and we have obtained the land of our people as an inheritance, we may all say in our humility: May the Lord be mindful of us.*

As Pharaoh fell, even though he had the power of horses and chariots on his side, so will the power of the "spiritual Pharaoh," variously interpreted as Satan and sinfulness, be covered over, giving Christians reason for singing joyful hymns. Collect 135 brings out the frequent theme of the land, bringing out a possible political interpretation, or indicating that "the land" is the kingdom of heaven.

Another phrase which appears in both Verecundus and the collects is *Jacob homo noster*, the former employing it in his commentary on the canticle in Deuteronomy.

> *CC* 93,33: *The spiritual Jacob, without a doubt a Christian man.*
> Collect 13: *...Jacob, our man, may exult in the flesh until, made Israel, he might merit to see you, God.*

Even though the wording does not match exactly, the sense is the same. In the collect, "Jacob" is the world, yet unconverted, which will be transformed into Israel, the Church. For Verecundus, Jacob is already Israel, for, being Christian, he understands the fullness of revelation.

Similar Themes

Thematic material in Verecundus also compares with that in the collects. Both bodies of work treat the Exodus theme in a like manner, consonant with the collect author's creation of a genre of "Exodus Psalms." The theme of the land also appears in both. Given the importance to North African Catholics of the property taken over by the Vandals and the episcopal presence of Donatists in even the smallest towns, this theme is to be expected in the writings of Catholics of the period.[19]

Even though there are other phrases and themes which appear in both Verecundus and the collects,[20] those treated above show the greatest affinity between the two, bringing out Brou's strongest arguments to attach the bishop of Junca to the *Africana* collects.[21]

Fulgentius of Ruspe

Despite Brou's advocacy of Verecundus, Fulgentius, in the end, seems to me the most likely author of the collects. Verecundus does not display the training in rhetoric and *sermo humilis* of his older contemporary. Nor does his writing indicate that he entered into the theological debates with Arians and Pelagians with the same relish as Fulgentius. Even though Verecundus's collection of passages for the proceedings of the Council of Chalcedon[22] includes the council's acceptance of the "Definition," he does not deal with christological themes in the collection. Fulgentius, on the other hand, vigorously defends orthodox christology throughout all of his works, including the collects.

In the important area of Christian rhetoric, Fulgentius of Ruspe's credentials are attested to by his biographer, Ferrandus, deacon of Carthage.[23] *Vita Fulgentii* appears in numerous manuscript copies, most of them from the ninth century, when Fulgentius's name appeared in the martyrologies. P. Lapeyre, the editor and French translator of the *Vita*, had located fifty copies by 1929, and believed that there were more.[24]

Fulgentius belonged to a senatorial family with land holdings in Carthage. His grandfather, Gordian, had fled Carthage during the Vandal migration across North Africa. His two sons returned, and, finding their home occupied, settled in the province of Byzacena, to the East of Carthage. One of them, Claudius, became the father of Fulgentius, who was born in the city of Thelepsis.[25]

An important influence on his early life and education was his mother, Marianna. She had him concentrate on Greek language and literature, forbidding any Latin authors. As a child, Fulgentius was able to recite all of Homer and a good portion of Menander. Such an insistence on classical Greek education also included training in grammar and rhetoric, and, after he had left behind his mother's strong influence, classical Latin as well.[26]

Fulgentius entered monastic life at an early age,[27] and soon became abbot. In 499, he fled from the Vandals to Sicily, with the intention of going to Egypt in order to live in the Thebaid desert, home of the great eremetical and cenobitical communities, but lived in a Roman monastery until 500, when he returned to Byzacena.[28]

Fulgentius was consecrated bishop in 503, and was soon exiled, along with sixteen other Byzacenan bishops, to Sardinia. During this first exile, he acted as secretary to the bishops' council, an office held by virtue of his youth as much as through his literary abilities.[29] Fulgentius became so adept at theological and political expression during this period that the Vandal king Thrasamund recalled him to Carthage in order to debate theology with him. During the periods at Ruspe, he kept to the life of the monk-bishop in the episcopal household. His extant theological works date from 515-527, from the two years after his first exile (515-517), through his second, which began in 517 and ended at Thrasamund's death in 523, and then until his own death at Ruspe.

Brou claims that Fulgentius's linguistic and theological affinity with the collects comes from his writings on the gratuity of grace.[30] In addition, Fulgentius employs the rare verb form *compluo*, as do the collects.[31] These similarities do not, in Brou's opinion, provide convincing evidence for Fulgentius's authorship. However, further literary and thematic analysis ties Fulgentius to the world of the collects more closely than Brou was willing to do. As a North African preacher, Fulgentius knew *sermo humilis*, and would have had ample opportunity to practice it. The contexts of the bishop Fulgentius's known writings, the arena of theological disputation, are different from the localized concerns of a monastery, yet the collects exhibit an understanding of theological and political concerns of an abbot whose thoughts went beyond the confines of the monastic walls. There is a strong possiblity that the abbot was the young Fulgentius.[32] Certainly, the tone of defiance against oppressors and the willingness to take positions on the theological controversies of the period mark the work of a young theologian and zealous champion of orthodoxy. Fulgentius did not begin his writing career with the carefully structured and argued works that date from 515.[33] By that time he had become the premier North African theologian of his generation.[34] Psalm collects offered an ideal genre in which to try out theological formularies and carry on the sort of theological conflict against the Arians to which his later works attest. Fulgentius's later career developed from these early experiences in expressing theological convictions. The passionate partisanship of the young abbot would not be acceptable on the stage of theological disputation, and was thus abandoned in favor of somber argumentation.

By comparing psalm verse interpretation in Fulgentius's works and the collects, one may see strong similarities. While Fulgentius's sermons, letters and treatises concentrate on doctrinal accuracy in a polemical context, the collects aim for the same sense of accuracy within the limitations of their genre.

Epistola 7 **and Collect 35**

The theme of the Samaritan in Lk. 10:30-37 as a type of the mercy of God receives treatment in both Fulgentius's *Epistola 7 ad Venantiam*and in collect 35. The epistle addresses correct penitence:

> *CC* 91,249: *Our Samaritan might never have carried the wounded man compassionately to the inn upon the beast if anyone might have perceived incurable wounds in him.*

The "incurable wounds" of sin are made curable by the salvific act of Christ, carrying the sins of the world in the suffering of his own body on the cross.

The collect, in spiritualizing Psalm 35, omits mention of the wounded man, but instead concentrates on the soteriological aspect of Jesus as Samaritan. Verse 7 of the psalm mentions salvation for people and beasts,[35] which leads Fulgentius to explain the meaning of the psalm's revelation in light of the gospel story. The resulting phrase is a bit clumsy:

> *For the Samaritan doctor of the world carried all of us on his own beast.*

Despite the awkwardness, due to the abridgement of thought required by the collect form, the collect teaches an orthodox and original interpretation of a familiar story to the community.

Augustine had used this interpretation earlier in a Sermon 171:

> *PL* 38,934: *...in which Samaritan he wished to perceive the Lord Jesus Christ himself.*

In receiving Augustinian theology, both Fulgentius's collect and epistle take two different approaches, the former to address a theological problem (Can beasts be saved?) within limited space, the latter to illustrate a teaching on the theme of conversion of life, an important element of penitence.[36]

Ad Thrasamundum and Collects 84 and 86

In a portion of this polemical work written at the request of the Vandal ruler, Thrasamund, Fulgentius address the orthodox position on the two natures of Christ by quoting Ps. 86:5:

> *CC* 91,113: *Mother Sion will say, 'Men are made in her, and the Most High himself has begotten her.'*

In the treatise, the psalm quotation and its interpretation follow a quotation from Jn. 1:1-2,14, an important text in Catholic-Arian disputations, and its interpretation, both of which affirm orthodox thought concerning the two natures. By implication, both accept the "Definition" of Chalcedon, which connects the *hypostases* of divinity with God and humanity with us. The expressive limitations of the genre produce some tortured phrasing in collect 86:

> *...so that, in him who as our God on earth was made human.*

However, in its paraphrase of Jn 1:14, the collect offers an unmistakable affirmation of orthodox christology, and an affinity with the anti-Arian polemics of *Ad Thrasamundum*.

During the course of his argument that Christ had a human, rather than a heavenly, body, Fulgentius quotes Ps. 84:10,12:

> *CC* 91:158-159: *...so that glory may live in our land, truth has been born from the land.*

The quotation is preceded by a quotation and interpretation taken from Jn. 3:13. The collect interpretation makes the same point as Fulgentius's treatise:

> *...so that your truth, which has been raised up in our land according to the flesh, may give sweetness to those who are consubstantial with it.*

The, once again, awkward phrasing serves theological purposes. By referring to "our land," there is the possibility of a political reference underneath the theological referents to humanity's biblical connection with land, something that Fulgentius wisely omits from his treatise addressing a Vandal ruler, as well as an affirmation of Chalcedonian orthodoxy.

Dicta regis Thrasamundi et contra ea responsionum

The *Dicta regis Thrasamundi*[37] uses more dialectic than *Ad Thrasamundum*, listing the king's objections to, and Fulgentius's defenses of, orthodox christology.[38]   Both Thrasamund and Fulgentius employ psalm verses in their arguments that also receive interpretation in the collects.

Objection 3 begins with a catena of scriptural verses in which Thrasamund offers texts that, in the Arian interpretation, point to a temporal beginning for the *logos*.[39] The one psalm verse in the list comes from Ps. 2:7: *The Lord said to me: you are my son; today I have begotten you.* According to the Arian interpretation, as the Father speaks in a temporal manner (*today I have begotten you*), this indicates that the Son is a created being. Fulgentius cleverly parries Thrasamund's objection with interpretations of Ps. 2:8 and Acts 13:32-33 (in which Paul quotes Ps. 2:7). For Fulgentius, *today I have begotten you*, refers to the day of the Resurrection and Jesus's position as the "first-born of the dead." Collect 2 indicates the same awareness of Arian interpretation of verse 7:

> *May you never permit the most evil demon to go through our lands, for the entire passion of human substance fell by lot to Christ, your Son, while he was providing himself with it in the Virgin.*

Heresy is compared to a ravaging demon, while the Incarnation receives a vivid interpretation that incidently affirms the teaching of the *Theotokos* as well as bringing in the theme of the Passion. The connection of "land" to "flesh," both threatened by evil, connects human flesh to the humanity of the only-begotten Son, who saved humanity through the existence of the two natures in one person. Without having the space to include the useful Acts text, the collect boldly draws attention to orthodox christological belief.

Earlier, in his response to Thrasamund's quotation of Prov. 8:22: *The Lord created me at the beginning of his ways; before the ages he begot me*, Fulgentius quotes Ps. 115:16: *I am your servant and the son of your handmaid.* He places both verses into the mouth of Christ, who proclaims the servitude of his human substance to the Father. Fulgentius holds that this proclamation supports, through its reference to the handmaid (the Virgin), indicates the created nature that the *logos* took upon himself, part of the divine plan for all ages, rather than indicating his birth in time, which is indicated by the second half of the proverb, using the term "begotten."[40] The collect for the psalm, which prays: *quickly destroy the bonds of the sons of your handmaid*, does not give a christological interpretation, identifying the handmaid as the Church and the monks as her sons. The beginning of the collect sets the personal tone: *Accept, Lord, the prayers of your household*. In this instance, the desire for each monk's personal salvation informs the collect.

Ad Monumum Libri III

Ad Monimum and *De remissione peccatorum* were written during Fulgentius's second exile to Sardinia (517-523). The first book of *Ad Monimum* defends the existence of two ways of predestination: glory or punishment. Chapter five,[41] which teaches that sin is not predestined by God, begins with Ps. 17:29: *Illumine my darkness*. After equating the light imagery of the psalm with the true light of God, Fulgentius proceeds to the subject of predestination, taking much of his argument from Augustinian theology. Collect 17 begins with a petition taken from the same verse: *Remove from us, Lord, the darkness of our sins, and illumine our hearts by the consubstantial light of your word*. Both works connect darkness with sin, but the treatise has the room and the aim to continue onto a philosophical discussion. The collect employs a christological theme, connecting the psalm with the light imagery of Jn. 1:9.

In chapter twenty-three of the same book of *Ad Monimum*,[42] Fulgentius asserts that God did not create evil, therefore no one is predestined to sin. He follows a quotation of Wis. 1:13: *God did not make death*, with a quotation from Ps. 10:8: *The Lord is just and loves justice; his face has seen justice*. Together they illustrate the holiness of God's creation as well as God's righteousness. The collect reacts to the verse in an anti-Pelagian manner: *made safe by the justice of your grace by which we have been saved by no preceding merits of our own*. By rejecting the claim of the psalm, that certain individuals are just, the collect changes the references to indicate that God alone is just. The treatise uses the wisdom and psalm verses in a larger context than does the collect, and the psalm verse can be used in order to make way for the larger discussion of grace and free will from an Augustinian context.

Ad Euthymium de remissione pecatorum

Two psalm quotations indicate that the collects and the treatise share sense of pastoral concern about the remission of sins. Fulgentius responds to requests for guidance by Euthymius, sent *from your heart,* in a manner both pastoral and theologically exacting. In his interpretation of Ps. 24:7: *Do not remember the sins of my youth and ignorance,*[43] Fulgentius evokes the prophetic utterance of David, ending his discussion of the divine gift of conversion of heart with the psalm quotation. The collect quotes the psalm almost exactly, characteristically changing the grammatical number from singular to plural.

Continuing in his pastoral mode, Fulgentius quotes Ps. 102:10-12: *He did not act toward us according to our sins, nor according to our injustices did he repay us; for as high as heaven is above the earth is his mercy over those who fear him; as far as east is from west, so far did he make our sins from us.*[44] The treatise quotes this with little comment, as a clear example from Scripture of God's mercy. The collect fashions verses eleven and twelve into a petition: *Arouse in us the word of this prophecy according to the height of heaven from earth. Confirm your mercy upon us, and make our sins as far from us as east is from west.* That both works chose to interpret the same verses of such a lengthy psalm offers significant connection between Fulgentius and the collects.

De ueritate predestinationis

Fulgentius wrote the three books on predestination to the presbyter John and the deacon Venerius while he was living in Ruspe after his second exile (523-527). The treatise allows Fulgentius greater space to make theological points than does the collect form, in this case an interpretation of Ps. 15:1: *Keep me Lord, for I have hoped in you.* Fulgentius writes: *But we might save our heart, if he will have saved us to whom is said: Keep me Lord, for I have hoped in you.*[45] The collect interprets the petition: *Keep us by your gratuitous grace.* The treatise uses this collect to begin a long discussion on the topic of gratuitous grace, but the collect is limited to one phrase.

Fulgentius continues his discussion with a scriptural catena which follows the theme of Ps. 15:1.[46] Of the various psalms in the list, Ps. 24:20: *Keep my soul, Lord, and free me,* receives treatment in its collect as well as in the treatise. Fulgentius places the verse in

David's mouth, following an injunction from Jer. 17:21: *Keep our souls*. The collect fashions the psalm verse into a double petition: *Keep our souls and free us, Lord, so that we who call upon you may not be confounded*. While the treatise goes on to connect the scripture quotations with an Augustinian approach to grace, the collect follows its petitions with two more petitions taken from the psalm: *May you not remember the sins of our youth and ignorance, but be mindful of us according to your mercy*, evoking Augustinian guidelines on making petition to the Lord.[47]

From the examples on the previous pages, one may see that thematic interpretation of the psalms indicate a connection between Fulgentius and the collects. Following Brou's example in his work on Verecundus, some illustrations of similar word usage follow.

Similar Vocabulary

Striking as the similar usage of the phrases *Pharaoh spiritalis* and *Jacob homo noster*, is between Verecundus and the collects, more shared phrases and words appear between Fulgentius and the collects. A brief listing follows:

Agricola:
  Sermo 1 (*CC* 91A, 891): *God is our farmer*.
  Collect 125: *For you are the farmer*.

Pastor et oues:
  Ad Thrasamundum (*CC* 91, 109-110): *Christ is our shepherd, of whom, as is testified by the authority of the Apostles, we are the sheep*.
  Collect 57: *Rise up and be present to defend the sheep for which the Good Shepherd laid down his life*.

Creatrix:
  This feminine form appears in *Sermo* 2 (*CC* 91A, 900), *Ad Thrasamundum* (*CC* 91, 120) and Collect 118.11.

Gratuitu munere:
  Epistola 14 (*CC* 91, 389), as well as Collects 10, 14, 113, 118.4 and 118.18 use this Augustinian term for "grace." *Gratuitus* appears in

Ad Monimum 1 (*CC* 91, 5), *Epistola* 14 (*CC* 91, 389; 437-38), *Epistola* 17 (*CC* 91A, 593), and Collects 10, 14, 15, 80, 96, 113, 118.4, 118.16, 118.18 and 141.

Pinguendo:
   Epistola 14 (*CC* 437): *The strength of grace is like fatty oil.*
   Collect 62: *Fill us, God, as it were, with riches and fat.*

The character of Pharaoh receives significant attention from the collect author, leading him to identify a genre of Exodus Psalms within the psalter. Fulgentius also makes much of the imagery of Pharaoh, exploiting the North African tradition of using biblical characters as political surrogates for the Vandal rulers,[48] and addresses the Exodus theme in a manner similar to the collects. *Sermo* 78 (*PL* 65, 950) states: *...the devil, who can be figuratively compared to Pharaoh*, and treats the surrogate tradition circumspectly, as his sermon was given in a public venue.

As the preceding examples indicate, the terms used by the young abbot Fulgentius in the collects continue to be used in his mature theological works, and indicate the development of his literary and rhetorical thought in the ten or twenty years between the collects and his treatises and sermons. Interpretations of grace remain constant in his works, and his theological interpretations of God as farmer, Christ as shepherd, references to *Creatrix* and the fatness of olive oil indicate that these images had an important role in his theological development as bishop and theologian.

His reference to Pharaoh in *Sermo* 78, similar to collect references, indicates a continuance of the practice of denouncing Vandal rulers through comparison with biblical villains.

Throughout his work, Fulgentius exhibits the qualities of good theological training, literary astuteness, pastoral concern and rhetorical ability which also appear in the collects. As a theologian, he broke no new ground, and, as a rhetorician, flashes of his technique are few. The *Africana* collects show the young abbot, ready to carry on the theological fight with color and vigor. Later, the bishop became sober and responsible, in the North African episcopal tradition. The need for theological orthodoxy tempered what might have been a sparkling literary career.[49]

CHAPTER 2

The Monastery of the Collects

Historical records of the monastery in which the *Africana* collects were composed have not come down to us. Yet, Fulgentius of Ruspe, in his role as teacher, exhorter and comforter, placed enough pertinent information into the collects that a partial account of the community's life can be posited. While conjecture is inevitable, the local specificity of the collects in theological matters can be profitably extended to include social and political matters as well. Even though he spiritualizes many of the references from the psalms, Fulgentius, as would any leader of a religious community, needed to address the daily lives of his monks, even during their prayer periods. Their life together had meaning in all of its aspects; each of their concerns were brought to prayer so that the community could bring their whole life together before the presence of God.

The Collect Manuscript and the Community's Psalter

The single manuscript of the *Africana* collects is the so-called *Psalter of Charlemagne*, preserved in the Bibliothèque National in Paris.[1] The volume includes a Gallican psalter, a litany of local saints, and orations after each psalm and each section of Psalm 118. Dom André Wilmart, who studied the psalter in the 1920's, identified the orations as being African in Origin. In 1949, Louis Brou published a critical edition of psalm collects that was partially based upon the work that his fellow Benedictine, Wilmart, had accomplished. He accepted Wilmart's classification and gave the collects found in the Paris psalter the title *Africana*.

The *Africana* collects appeared in the psalter as a part of Charlemagne's campaign to bring liturgical texts into his kingdom. His sources for such texts were Spain, Gaul and Italy. The North African collects came through one of the three sources to a scriptorium in the kingdom where they were copied into a psalter.

The Psalter of Charlemagne

Three psalters bear the title, *Psalter of Charlemagne*, one in Vienna,[3] another in Oxford,[4] and the one under consideration in Paris. Neither the Vienna nor the Oxford psalters includes collects.

As the prayers in the psalter following the litanies of the saints refer to Charles as king of the Franks and Lombards, and not emperor,[5] its probable date of production has been posited as between 795 and 800. The psalter contains no hymns or antiphons. Each psalm commences with a large initial letter fashioned into a fanciful animal shape,[6] and is preceded by a title and followed by a collect. A marginal note inscribed in a triangle accompanies each psalm. Biblical canticles, the litanies, and other prayers are included at the end, as well as a few miscellaneous antiphons and hymn fragments.[7]

After Psalm 108, there is a simple drawing of an aureoled Christ with an angel in attendance on either side. The figures have long noses, large eyes, cleft chins and plain, serious mouths. Each angel carries a cross. The drawing appears to have been a later addition, indicating that the book was used at some point after its initial production.[8] Red pigment appears as coloring throughout much of the psalter. Bright yellow pigment appears in the illumination at Psalm 133, and continues until Psalm 137, resuming at Psalms 142 and 143.

E. A. Lowe's description of the psalter agrees with Wilmart's conclusions concerning its Carolingian provenance. He adds further information concerning the physical aspects of the book. He notes that the parchment of the volume is rather thick, and that the black or brown ink has begun to scale off on the flesh sides. The script of the psalter is Carolingian miniscule of a late type. Corrections in a second hand occur in the same style. Wilmart's analysis of the script led him to conclude that the psalter was copied in northeastern France, possibly the scriptorium of St. Omer, by someone other than a Benedictine scribe. In addition to his published work on the psalter, Lowe sent a note to Brou in September, 1947, which the latter publishes in his study. In it, Lowe affirms Wilmart's conclusions concerning the place of copying due to the names of local saints mentioned in the litanies.[9] However, J. M. Casas, in his study of the *Africana* collects, posits the abbeys of Corbie or Saint-Riquier as possible copying venues.[10]

The single manuscript of the *Africana* collects did not survive the centuries unscathed, but its condition is remarkable, considering the treatment which it must have endured. Several of the vellum pages have been torn and sewn together. There is a lacuna between Psalms 4 and 6, with Psalm 5 missing completely. Another missing page results in the loss of the end of Psalm 148, its collect, and Psalm 149 and the beginning of its collect. Other portions of the manuscript have faded, resulting in the partial loss of collects 1 (which appears to be an erasure), 52, 131 and 144. Brou felt confident enough to reconstruct some words in collect 52, but lacunae remain in the rest.

Many of the collects contain copyist's abbreviations, as well as corrections by two other hands.[11] Such editorial additions correct mostly single letters, prepositions and other minor details.[12]

The appearance of psalm collects in the text gives rise to questions as to the psalter's actual purpose. In the late eighth century, the practice of reciting psalm collects was, at best, limited. The extent to which the text was used in a setting of communal prayer is open to question. Perhaps it was created to be a work for personal devotion.

The Collects for Psalm 118

The question of the psalter's organization of the collects is complicated by the apportioning of collects to Psalm 118. Even though the collects are alphabetized in imitation of the psalm, the first two collects take their inspiration from the first stanza of the psalm (*aleph*). The next twenty collects proceed from the second stanza (*beth*) to the twenty-second (*shin*), but do not refer to the twentieth stanza (*resh*). In the *Psalter of Charlemagne*, the collects for stanzas twenty and twenty-two (*shin* and *taw* respectively), are reversed in their order. The psalter incorporates the second collect for Psalm 118 in the second stanza, the third collect in the third stanza, and so on. As a result, after stanza 1, none of the collects is placed with its proper stanza. This odd feature would have limited the psalter's value for public liturgical use.

The Community's Psalter

The collects quote the psalms extensively. The psalter text used by the *Africana* community somewhat resembles the psalter used by Augustine, identified by Giovanni Bianchini as the *Psalter of Verona*,[13] which he edited in the eighteenth century.[14] The source of this psalter remains a subject of some conjecture. Paul Capelle, whose work on African Psalters remains an important contribution to the topic, synthesized scholarly discussion concerning *Ver.*, and concluded that previous studies could not ascertain whether Augustine's psalter was one he brought over from Italy or one of African origin. As an introduction to his own contribution to the discussion, Capelle proposes that Augustine would not have used a text for his sermons other than the one used by the people, and that the text of *Ver.* was the psalter in daily use in Hippo at the time.[15]

Capelle follows the synthesis with his own analysis of the texts of several psalters, including *Ver.* He concludes that *Ver.* is undoubtedly African. It employs vocabulary that appears in other psalters of unquestionable African origin.[16] Its textual peculiarities distinguish it from the two versions of the Latin psalter in general use at the time in Europe, the Roman and Gallican Psalters.

A dissenter in this field is J. M. Casas, whose study concludes that there is not enough evidence to unequivocally conclude that the psalter used in the collects is African in origin.[17]

With respect to Casas's opinion, I have found that the psalm quotations, which the collect author used in his orations, to be very similar to *Ver.* and other Africana psalters, and, one may assume, date back to fifth-century North Africa.

Temporal Concerns of the Monastery

The Vandal Presence

The Vandal migration from Jutland took the Germanic tribe down into Spain, and, from there, into North Africa. They won military victories against the Roman armies that protected the region, and made a steady progress to the East. In the course of his siege of Hippo, where Augustine lay dying, in 435, Gaiseric was offered and accepted a *foedus* from the empire. He probably received the provinces of northern Numidia, western Africa Proconsularis and most of Mauritania Sitifensis. This pact did not satisfy the Vandals for long, for, in October, 439, Gaiseric attacked Carthage. One year later he was in Sicily. At this point, Gaiseric accepted a new *foedus* from the empire which added Byzacena and Tripolitana to his holdings. The agreement fixed the borders of what was to become the Vandal kingdom, and most of the Vandals took up residence in Africa Proconsularis.[18]

Vandal occupation placed North Africa into a state of shock. Their Arianism, as well as their military presence, resulted in polemical writings and general condemnation on the part of Catholic authors.

Victor of Vita lamented the destruction of the countryside, appropriation of agricultural products and destruction of Churches by the Vandals. He characterized them as criminals, enemies of the sort bemoaned in Ps. 73:5-7, which he quotes in his *Historia Persecutionis*:

> *(they are) like woodmen in the forest; they have plied their axes, brought it down with pick and mallet, to the ground; they have set fire to your sanctuary, sullied the dwelling place of your glory in the dust.*[19]

Ulfilas, the monk from Constantinople who converted the Goths and, by extension, other Germanic tribes, introduced them to the Arian version of Christianity.[20] From the Germanic point of view, there was nothing particularly attractive about Arian, as opposed to Catholic, christology, which, in any event, with the known exception of Thrasamund, they did not study with any thoroughness, nor did the liturgical practices attract them. The practice of worshipping in the vernacular, which made Arianism more accessible than the Latin liturgy of the Catholics, was a prime attraction. Freedom from the language of Rome aided the Germans in asserting their independence and their own sense of identity, and gave them a feeling of immunity to assimilation into the Roman way of life, too long held up to them as superior to theirs.[21]

When they arrived in North Africa, the Vandals entered a world where Roman aristocratic life, however impoverished, still flourished, and the presence of landed gentry provided a strong reminder of the opportunistic *foedera* offered by a disintegrating Roman power structure as a means of keeping the Germanic tribes docile. After taking over the old senatorial holdings, all that was left to the Romans as a mode of expression was their religion. As a result, when the Vandals attempted to fit their cult of leadership and domination into a North Africa already suffering from a surfeit of castes, they found the Romans highly resistant, and the Berber tribes, who had a new enemy to raid, bothersome.

The replacement for the loss of the effectiveness of the cult of royal personality was Arian/Catholic strife. North African Catholics, well-versed in theological warfare after years of disputes with Donatists, the Vandals found an opponent with reserves of spiritual strength. Catholics had an impressive store of theological weapons with which to fight the military superiority of the Vandals and their social and political brutality. In the end, their stubborn adherence to Catholic teaching successfully resisted the Vandal policy of converting all of the subjects to Arianism. Arianism, however, was merely the occasion for conflict, Germanic reaction to the longtime hegemony of Rome being the actual cause.[22]

Within the Arian Church, the king exerted control over the Metropolitan of Carthage, naming bishops, calling synods, and assigning Arian clergy to churches.[23] Catholics would not accept such authority from a heretical ruler, and Gaiseric, who ruled from 428-477, responded with persecution. Catholic bishops, whose sheer numbers made them effective leaders of Roman society,[24] and, thus, a challenge to the unity which Vandals expected to center upon the king, were his first target; many were exiled to Sicily and Sardinia.

As for the monasteries, there is little testimony concerning their treatment, though foundations of women seem to have been a particular target of Vandal hostility.[25] Among the more lurid reports of Vandal cruelty in Victor of Vita's work were the martyrdoms, especially that of seven monks from Capsa that appears in his *Historia*, and in the anonymous *Passio septem monachorum*.[26] King Huneric's (477-484) proclamation of February 24, 484 forbade new cenobitical institutions,[27] but the decree was either ignored or overturned by those subsequent Vandal rulers who had more tolerance or more desire to curry favor with the Roman emperor in Constantinople.[28] During the exiles of Catholic bishops, priests, monks, and civil servants to Sardinia, small monastic communities grew and flourished on that island.[29]

The Vandals in the Collects

The rhetoric of the *Africana* collects includes references to the hardships of Vandal rule. Fulgentius's reception of the psalms helps to bring about a catharsis, touching the monks' concerns over the spiritual dangers under which they lived, and its secular appearance in the form of the occupation forces.

The numerous references to enemies[30] testify to the monastery's experience of oppression, both spiritual and physical. The terms used refer to various facets of enemy power, all of which is placed before God by the community in their prayer.

Spiritualized references to *hostis* center upon the devil, clearly characterized as such,[31] and as "demon,"[32] and "ancient enemy."[33] Spiritualized, *inimicus* indicates the "enemy of humankind,"[34] and the "enemy of our nature," the sinner.[35]

In their other appearances, *hostis* and *inimicus* retain a sense of ambiguity, forming an interpretative tension between temporal and spiritual meanings. The collects urge the monks to meditate upon the injustice of their situation as heirs to sin, which results in the poverty of their souls as well as their temporal and social poverty as politically disenfranchised people. Collect 82 states:

> *Your enemies acted against the covenant, Lord . . . make your enemies like dung of the earth, who wanted to possess your altar for themselves.*

Fulgentius here exploits the Psalmist's claim that Israel's enemies are also God's.[36] That the collect includes the violent image of dung from the psalm imparts a sense of the social turbulence caused by the monks' enemies. There seems to be a sort of call to arms here, a petition for a societal change that will reform that which the enemies have overthrown.

Other uses of the term *inimicus* remain unclear as to whether they indicate spiritual or temporal enemies. Four references[37] appear in the context of realized salvation, requesting deliverance from enemies. The usage recalls the "reminder" portion of the lament psalm.[38] Collect 76, in the midst of its petitions, proposes: *If all our enemies anticipated the vigils*, taken from verse 5 of the psalm: *my eyes anticipate the vigils*. Whether the reference is to the demons of the night or to some military action of the Vandal army, sent to harass the monks, remains unknown. Collect 126 seeks protection:

> *Look down, Lord, and guard, so that, what cannot be guarded in us unless you guard (it); build what cannot be finished unless you build it, so that we, having become your inheritance in all things, might not be confounded while they will speak with your enemies at the gate.*

The verb *custodio*[39] (to guard), connected with *aedifico* (to build) indicates a state of siege. Confrontation with enemies is taking place in the context of a sort of negotiation of dialogue in which the monks take part from within the safety of the monastery, or from within the safety of theological orthodoxy. The very physicality of the image adds to the spiritual dimensions at its heart. The building does not make the monastery; the community of believers forms the structural material, and God's presence as builder protects the members as they deal with heresy or temporal power from the outside.

Iniquus appears as a substantive in a thematic pocket (a consecutive series of collects which treat the same theme using similar vocabulary), collects 118.16 and 118.17, and remains ambiguous in both. The second of the two collects states: *the evil ones have destroyed your law*. The Arian Vandals qualify as destroyers of the law of love among Christians, and, as such, are in opposition to the petition of the collect 119.16: *grant us to love your law and hate the evil ones*. The psalm's theme is the Torah of God, and the stanzas contain the terms "law" and "evil ones,"[40] but the monks would be able to identify specific "evil ones" for themselves.

Malignus (evildoer) appears in collect 25: *congregations of evildoers*, and collect 63: *assembly of evildoers*, and indicates massed groups. the Vandals being likely candidates in a temporal interpretation. Collect 25 also refers to *men of blood*, implying the destructive power of the evildoers. The stories of the martyrdoms could well evoke this epithet. Collect 95 asks God to rise up against evildoers, and not to desert, *the shepherds of your flock*. Implied here is active struggle, with an oblique reference to bishops as shepherds, both those who are in exile, or those who eluded the Vandals and secretly continued to lead their congregations, even going so far as to hold clandestine synods, such as the one in 502.[41]

An atmosphere of occupation naturally leads to expressions of persecution. In collect 7, the persecutors act in consort with *the most evil demon* in order to take God's gift from the community, and collect 141 bemoans their apparent strength. In collect 118.22, the persecutors (acting without cause) are identified as "princes," thus adding a daring reference to the Vandal kings. Before its petition to be saved from these princes, the collect asks: *may we always exult in your words as one who has found much spoil*, a clear military reference taken from verse 162 of the psalm.

In addition to the reference to princes, two other collects go as far as is prudently possible to identify oppressors. Collect 53 asks for God to: *convert the insurrection of the aliens*, and collect 143 asks to be saved from *alien sons*. Taken together, collects 53, 118.22 and 143, spread out among the collects, are as close as one comes in the orations to openly condemning the Vandal occupation. By employing God's word in the context of military spoil, the identity of the victor is no secret. As the Arians have misused biblical texts to promote their heresy, they have stolen the true meaning of the Word. God will restore it, as well as the land, to Catholic North Africa as soon as the occupation is over.

References to the Vandal occupation appear spread out among the collects. Any visitor to the monastery would not necessarily take the references as social commentary, while the monks who lived with the collects and the psalms could internalize them and make any applications they wished in their personal meditation. Thus, Fulgentius addresses their concerns without unduly taking their attention away from spiritual matters.

Some enemies are clearly supernatural, and the collects attest to the prevalent belief in demons,[42] and the avoidance of the evil eye[43] and the evil tongue. [44]

Vandal Policy and the Compositional Date of the Collects

The vehemence of the references to persecution and enemies that appear to be directed towards the Vandals indicate that Fulgentius composed his orations during a period of intensified persecution. Attention to such topics by occupied populations does not occur during periods of tranquility, when people turn to their daily concerns and prepare for the next round of sanctions. The ebb and flow of Vandal policy, and its effect in royal programs to control or eliminate Catholic influence, frame the compositional period of the collects.

Three periods of renewed or intensified persecution occurred during the reigns of the Vandal kings after the initial measures of Gaiseric, which began in 436. As Brou dates the collects to the late fifth century,[45] the later periods of persecution, rather than the initial one, correspond to his dating. Gaiseric himself renewed anti-Catholic action after a period of comparative laxity, following the death of the Catholic bishop Deogratias of Carthage (456 or 457). Huneric, who had shown leniency, began persecution in 482, followed by the anti-Catholic proclamations of 484.[46] Thrasamund, while inclined to the use of persuasion rather than of force, nevertheless exiled bishops to Sardinia in 502, while, during the same year, the remaining bishops met secretly to plan their resistance.[47] Collect 93, with its praise of the courage of "shepherds," seems to offer a bit of testimony to this meeting, and thus situates the composition of the collects to 502, when the religio-political climate had become dangerous for Catholic bishops.

War and Armaments

Of the six collects that mention war,[48] four contain the phrase, *bellum spiritalis nequitiae*.[49] Fulgentius employs the phrase in various ways in the collects. Collect 28 expresses the belief that the forces of evil have not yet won their battle against the Church. In order to continue fighting the battle, however, help is needed, and is requested in collect 75's petition to God to allow the Christ, *he who was made known in Judea*, to remove war, and collect 23's confidence in Christ's ability to settle this war. Collect 147 petitions God the Father to the same end. These do not appear in thematic pockets.

More ambiguous use of the theme of war appears in collect 119, which follows its petition for deliverance of souls from *unjust lips* with a petition for a safeguard against war waged by those who hate peace, and collect 150's combined petition against war and schism.[50] This petition brings out the clearest commentary on war in the collects connected with the Arian Vandals.

All of the references to armaments: sword,[51] shield,[52] bow,[53] and arrows,[54] appear in the psalm texts and receive spiritual interpretations. The enemies to be fought with these weapons are Satan, sin and spiritual evil. In collect 37, as in its (penitential) psalm, arrows are directed towards the sinner. As their source is the just wrath of God, they do not appear in connection with war imagery.[55]

Political Themes

Land

Even though references to land are spiritualized, the theme carries political and economic significance to monks who grew up in this agricultural area. Thirteen collects use the term *terra* in various contexts.[56] An historical reference to deliverance from the land of Egypt appears in collect 80 and collect 150 contains an agricultural reference to land. Collect 84 employs the term to affirm Christ's human nature, in connection, of course, with his divine nature: *your truth, which has been raised up in our land according to the flesh* .

The political aspects of land receive some subtle attention in collect 45, which evokes the Vandal occupation in its declaration of faith: *Lord, we will not fear when our land is disturbed*, and collect 135's claim: *we have obtained the land of our people as an inheritance.* Fulgentius also offers an astute observation of the religio-political aspect of land in verse 21 of the psalm: *(God) gave their land as an inheritance.* In his interpretation, the Promised Land of the Israelites now becomes the occupied land of North Africa, what is now "their" (i.e., the Vandals') land will become "our" land once more, as part of God's plan.

Fatherland

In his three references to *patria*[57] in the collects, Fulgentius chooses an eschatological interpretation that depoliticizes a term which could easily become overtly nationalistic. Collects 104 and 109 petition for membership in the *patria eterna*, further requesting, respectively, leadership out of Egypt, (either a spiritualized Egypt or the "Egypt" of Vandal occupation) and domination in the midst of enemies. Even though eschaton and judgment are the focus of his allusions, ignoring the political aspects of the term *patria* is difficult, especially given the references to Egypt and domination in the two collects. Despite the spiritual side of the interpretation, any political leanings of the monks must have received some sense of affirmation in their meditation on these psalms through the texts of the collects. Collect 118.4 further adds a political touch by requesting that the community be made *citizens of the heavenly fatherland.*

Insurrection

Insurrection as a political force receives attention in collect 53, and collect 16 addresses its spiritual aspects. The former sees the *aliens* as insurrectionists, thus referring to the Vandal presence. Collect 16 petitions:

> *Lord, protect your people under the shadow of your wings from the face of the hostile ones who plan an insurrection against our soul.*

The two collects complement each other in a manner which illustrates Fulgentius's goal to offer both spiritual and temporal comfort to his monks. By removing the term "insurrection" from the political arena in collect 16, he heightens the sense of the danger that they all face, for danger to the body is not as deadly as that to the soul.

Agricultural and Economic Concerns

Agriculture

Even the most spiritually oriented writer must make references that his audience can recognize as part of its own daily experience. From the evidence offered in the collects, the temporal occupation of the monastery appears to have been agriculture. Even during the Vandal occupation, Latin North Africa, formerly one of the breadbaskets of the Roman Empire (Egypt being another), still produced the comestible glories that grace Mediterranean tables, despite Victor of Vita's lament over a ravaged countryside.[58] The residents, including monks, continued to work the land and bring forth crops.

A more objective view of contemporary farming practices than Victor of Vita's appears in a series of economic records called the Albertini Tablets. The records appear on 45 small planks of wood, recorded by five or six scribes, some of which were discovered by North Africans in 1928, near the modern town of Tabessa. Eugene Albertini found the rest, and dated them to the reign of king Gunthamund (493-496).[59] Christian Courtois's study of the tablets[60] shows them to be a series of private sector agricultural transactions. Some of the same localized Latin word forms appear in the collects.[61]

In testimony to the importance of olives to the region, the tablets refer to dealings with them 178 times, far more than the other crops of figs, almonds, or pistachios.[62] Although the collects' two references to olive trees[63] and two to oil[64] appear in their respective psalms, and are spiritualized in their collects, Fulgentius could not have failed to exploit such a pervasive food product in his collects, certainly part of the monks' diet. His references to the *oil of charity* addresses the messianic theme as well as the duty of love each monk owed to his brothers.

Also spiritualized from their appearances in psalm texts, yet, testifying to the agricultural occupation of the monks, are references to: fruits,[65] grain,[66] sowing and reaping,[67] the eternal storehouse,[68] God as farmer,[69] wine,[70] rain,[71] dung,[72] seeds and their germination,[73], planting,[74] cultivation,[75] flowering,[76] bread,[77] and hunting.[78] There is also a reference in collect 62 to *riches and fat* in a simile comparing them to the riches of God's grace. Collect 56's reference to planting places the term *plantauit* in association with *infestantium* in its text:

> *Look down upon those whom your right hand has planted...protect us . . . until the iniquity of our vexatious (infestantium) sins has passed by.*

While *infestantium* does not refer explicitly to disease, comparison of the blight of sin to that of plants is invited by the proximity of the two terms.

References to rain in collects 65 and 150 do not spiritualize the term as do collects 66 and 67. The thematic pocket of collects 65-67 in which *rain* appears brings out Fulgentius's practice of addressing both temporal and spiritual matters in the collects. The temporal importance of favorable climactic conditions to the community is made more specific due to the fact that neither Psalm 65 nor 150 contain any explicit reference to rain.

The imagery of collect 125 is completely agricultural:

May the seeds of justice germinate in your sight. We sow these seeds with tears in your sight so that we might weep with joy what we await in patience, since you are the farmer.

Taking its inspiration from verses 5-6 of the psalm, the collect presents a sketch of the spiritual life, from the sowing of the *iusticie semina* to their harvest. The image of farmer, possibly quaint to modern eyes, serves to connect the gospel story of the sower (*seminat*),[79] to the admonition in the Letter of James:

Behold, the farmer (agricola) waits for the precious fruit of the earth, being patient over it until it receives the early and the late rain.[80]

The letter's reference to rain mirrors the tears of the psalm and the collect. Fulgentius here creates a meditative gem, pulling together three scriptural texts that affirm both the manual occupation of the monks and their spiritual salvation.

Economic Concerns

All references to economic matters in the collects come from the psalm texts themselves and receive spiritualized interpretations in their collects.

Five collects refer to the poor,[81] and allow Fulgentius to treat both the pecuniary and spiritual aspects of poverty. He identifies the poor as belonging to God,[82] and connects them with petitions to God to save them from their condition; Collect 131 specifically asks that they be *sated with bread.* No connection is made with temporal or spiritual poverty of the monastery itself, as the poor are always referred to in the third person. The collects thus teach the monks charity, challenging them to identify with all poor people everywhere, and not just those in close proximity to the monastery.

Three references to precious substances: treasure,[83] gold and silver,[84] and gold and chrysolite,[85] appear in the collects and denote spiritual treasure. Gospel texts serve as inspiration,[86] pointing out the perfection of revelation in the light of Christ, and identifying the only real treasure.

Collect 14 contains puzzling references to money and usury:

> *...make us through gratuitous gift to be inhabitants of the eternal tabernacle.*
> *Let us never take money from the innocent. Grant to our littleness to give*
> *money to the moneylenders, and may you not demand this back with interest,*
> *but with crowns which are gratuitous gifts.*[87]

Ps. 14:2 identifies the first of those who *shall sojourn in (the Lord's)*
tent as those who practice economic honesty towards others, and this
quality becomes the focal point of the collect, providing a frame for
Fulgentius's message. The collects contain frequent references to the
community's desire for the Lord's house,[88] but the petition that they
not practice usury does not seem to fit in with monastic practice at all.
Patrick Verbracken's rendering: *let us never accept presents for the*
loss of the innocent,[89] may indicate his sense that the monastery ought
not take gifts from those who had little of their own, especially for the
promise of prayers on the donors' behalf. The interest God would
exact from such money would be punishment for the monastery's sin
of greed.

Collect 150 as Thematic Summary

Collect 150 is the culmination of the *Africana* series, as is its psalm
for the psalter. The political, agricultural, and spiritual themes that
have heretofore occupied Fulgentius throughout the compositional
process receive attention in this final oration:

> *With well-sounding cymbals out of love for God and neighbor, we greatly*
> *praise you, God Almighty Father, in your saints, in the firmament of your*
> *power, for you are found with difficulty where you are, but with greater*
> *difficulty where you are not. Be merciful to your people, we beg. Change the*
> *mourning of all into rejoicing. Direct our hearts. Cure the wounds of all.*
> *Forgive the sins of all. Grant also rain to your land in its own time. Avert your*
> *anger from us. Grant abundance to your people. Suppress war and heresies.*
> *Extinguish schism everywhere, so that we may be helped with divine*
> *consolation in all things and through all things, and our spirits might praise*
> *you always.*

Some puzzling imagery appears in the collect. The assertion that there
are places in which God *is not* seems to negate the famous testimony
of Psalm 138 and its collect. Is Fulgentius suggesting that God is
absent from the hearts of sinners? Even in those souls where God is
present, the need for full attention to prayer must be fulfilled before

God's presence reveals itself. The reference to curing can indicate either physical or spiritual wounds, and is the one medical reference in the collects. The following petition asking for forgiveness of sins does not clarify the matter.[90]

The phrase, *well-sounding cymbals out of love for God*, calls to mind Paul's reference to a *clanging cymbal* as being bereft of love, even though one *speak with the tongues of men and angels*.[91] The monastic community sees their prayer as being filled with love, and therefore well-sounding.

The agricultural portion of the collect uses a petition against God's anger to connect two temporal ideas, rain and abundance. Even though the collects are primarily spiritual, Fulgentius does not forget that God's wrath can take meteorological forms.

For the rest of the collect, Fulgentius addresses the religio-political situation. Heresy, schism, and war appear together, implying the military might and Arian beliefs of the Vandals. By employing a series of curt petitions, he refers to the Vandal presence with more clarity than he has shown throughout the other collects.

CHAPTER 3

Psalm Reception and the Collects

Latin Psalm Reception and Fulgentius

Fulgentius approached the psalms in an interpretative tradition that developed within the genre of the exegetical treatise, treating the entire psalter. Interestingly, the earliest influence on Latin writers in this genre comes from Origen, as translated by Rufinus.[1] His spiritual, allegorical exegesis[2] influenced the psalm commentaries of Hilary of Poitiers,[3] who approached the psalms as prefigurations of Christ's life. Hilary's Prologue, with its discussion of the meanings of the various "houses" (i.e., each individual psalm), each with its own "key" (interpretation), employs Origenic mysticism.

Ambrose's homilies on the psalms[4] also incorporate Origen's method by highlighting the prophetic character of David's authorship,[5] and by finding in the psalms a spiritual sense that he interprets tropologically.[6] Augustine recounts Ambrose's influence on his reading of the Hebrew Scriptures in his *Confessions*.[7]

Jerome's homilies on the psalms apply allegorical method with the pastoral mood that befits homilies. He employs *sermo humilis*, and pays attention to daily life and communal interaction in a way that is similar to Fulgentius in the collects.

Augustine's pastoral care for the people in Hippo combined with a well-organized philosophical and theological perspective, characterizes his *Enarrationes in Psalmos*. He addresses the psalms within a liturgical context, as does Fulgentius, as each psalm he treats had just been sung before the homily. A theological outlook, honed through years of conflict with Manichaeans, Donatists, Arians and Pelagians, and an effective use of *sermo humilis*, bring out his main rhetorical theme: the importance of the revelation of the psalms to the mission of the Church.

Allegorically, the divisions of the psalter, far from suggesting genres as they do for modern scholars (and, in the case of Exodus themes, to Fulgentius), signify for Augustine the various spiritual experiences of Christ's interior prayer and, by extension, Christ's Church. The full revelation of Christ in the Christian Scriptures enabled Augustine to clearly focus on the partial revelation available in the psalms. He takes a scholarly approach, spending time explaining to the people the differences between their Latin versions and the Septuagint from which they were translated, providing the clearest exegesis possible.[9]

Fulgentius is an heir of Origen's spiritual exegetical method, as he generally eschews the literal sense of the text in favor of an applied spirituality. Allegorical method does not appear much in the collects, as the form offers little space for developing allegorical themes, however, some of his imagery hints at a reception in an allegorical mode. Fulgentius's treatises do address allegorical interpretations of Scripture, although intermittently, as his interest lights more upon theological matters rather than biblical exegesis.

Fulgentius's Genre Shift

Departing from the Latin tradition of commentaries and homilies as the basis for his interpretation, Fulgentius shifted genres from commentary to collect. Like Augustine, he related to the psalter within the sphere of Christ's revelation and to its importance as a pastoral tool for his community. Unlike Augustine, he does not have the opportunity to treat every verse. His verse choices reflect, above all, his pastoral concerns. Each verse chosen embodies a lesson for the community's spiritual and temporal experiences. The collect's petitions, emerging from those chosen verses, shifts the tradition of psalm interpretation. While allegory, Christian fulfillment, polemic, Church and the whole people of God appear in the collects, the concerns are localized in order that the orations, and thus the psalms, may become the most efficient spiritual guides possible for this particular monastic community.

Reception Devices

Reception

Fulgentius's rhetorical training, so little used in his treatises, appears occasionally in the collects. Brou correctly states that, on the surface, the collects are not rhetorical gems. He notes the "lack of elegance," and the "short phrases, each following the other without rhetorical link."[10] Within the bounds of his community's experience, however, Fulgentius does employ rhetorical technique with a degree of subtlety, possibly necessitated by the presence of Vandal sympathizers, creating austere prayers with an energetic advocacy of the theological and social concerns of the monastery.

As a Christian of his period, Fulgentius believes that the psalms are a shadow of the complete revelation brought about in Christ. Frequent address to the Lord as "almighty" and "eternal," and evocations of Christ as "Son" illustrate this belief. His concern for the Christian education of his monks dictates his use of hermeneutic bridges: psalm verses and material from the Gospels and Epistles.

Mimesis

In order for the monks to better receive the psalms, Fulgentius places them within the reference points of the North African monastic church.[11] He exploited the drama and spirituality of the psalter, exchanging, in most chases, the world of the senses for that of the spirit.[12] At times, he allows the psalter to speak for itself without taking any further creative action. Portions of the psalter are quoted verbatim, and other portions are paraphrased closely.[13] Reception of verses as they appear is interspersed with mimetic interpretation within the collects.

Catharsis

Monastic life under the Vandals and intense theological conflict from several quarters must have produced considerable tension among the monks. Fulgentius's orations offer a cathartic release of the tension, mirroring the ultimate release of all earthly concerns in the salvation offered by Christ.

The psalms themselves offer catharsis in their praise of God for actions of salvation, expressions of anger at spiritual and temporal enemies, and expressions of intense love for God. In transferring that catharsis to the collect, Fulgentius interprets the psalms as vehicles of comfort and hope. An important hermeneutic bridge is the spiritual and temporal suffering of his monks. Emotional release and affirmation of their proper Catholic beliefs come from an assurance of a hearing from God, confidently assumed by the collects.[14]

The three rhetorical movements of reception, mimesis, and catharsis, whether employed consciously by Fulgentius or not, form the compositional basis of the *Africana* collects. Brou recognized the decline of classical Latin style in his criticisms of the dry, abrupt phrasing found in the collects, but that same phrasing leads one to appreciate what rhetorical style there is, particularly that of *sermo humilis*.

The collects affirm the belief that, in Christ, all things are made new, and appeal to a "least common denominator" that all of the monks had experienced, and this causes the words of Scripture to take on new meanings through the directed meditation of a collect. There is no need for classical oratory among those who contemplate the mysteries of Christ.

A Twentieth Century Interpretative Tool

A valuable structure in which to frame a literary/rhetorical study of psalm reception is Herman Gunkel's landmark study, *Einleitung in die Psalmen*.[15] Gunkel's classifications (hymns of praise, laments, thanksgiving psalms, royal psalms, and wisdom psalms), are useful in that they offer a series of headings under which one may compare and contrast the ways in which the North African monastic community received certain psalms.

In order to provide samples of Fulgentius's reception of psalm theme, this chapter will investigate Gunkel's genres of hymns of praise, royal psalms and wisdom psalms. The lament genre, under which the majority of the psalms fall, is too immense to include in this brief study; however, reception techniques remain constant throughout the collect series in all of Gunkel's genres.

In addition to the classifications offered by Gunkel, Fulgentius himself delineates two psalm genres: Exodus Psalms and Penitential Psalms. His collects identify a sense of genre reception and identification of collections within the psalter. The Penitential Psalm collects help to further trace this interpretative tradition back to Augustine.

Modes of Reception

Fulgentius receives psalm texts in various manners. Most often, he fashions a petition from one or more verses of the given psalm. In other places he employs vocabulary from the psalm and offers an interpretation that can be identified in light of reception, mimesis and catharsis. Christian allegorical and eschatological imagery spiritualize the psalm message. In some instances, large portions of a collect address soteriological matters, and the Augustinian exegetical technique of seeing Christ in the psalms also appears.

With the possible exception of the Penitential Psalms, Fulgentius does not interpret each psalm as a complete entity. He culls verses for their value as teaching tools within a liturgical reception.[16] Despite this approach, some of the genres identified by Gunkel do receive interpretation which apply to the genres he identifies, particularly the hymns of praise, royal psalms, and wisdom psalms. The following investigation of Fulgentius's reception will concentrate on Gunkel's categories of hymns of praise, royal psalms and wisdom psalms, and of Fulgentius's genres of Exodus Psalms and the Penitential Psalms.

Petitions in the Collects

Virtually all of the collects include petitionary prayer requesting grace, deliverance or some other favor from God. In composing petitions, Fulgentius generally appropriates a statement from the psalm and incorporates its vocabulary into the petition. Many petitions lead to an *ut* or *quod* clause, which declares the efficacious result of divine intervention. Material from the psalm may also appear in these clauses.

Petitions form the customary cathartic bridge between the psalm text and the monastic community. A sense of urgency emerges. God must act soon, in a sure and powerful manner. Such emotional content results from the persecution under which the community lived. The collects impart the hope of being heard, and indicate that the community carried on its liturgical life in the context of that hope.

The Collects for the Hymns of Praise

Psalter hymns generally open with joyous expressions of praise, frequently "Hallelujah." The enthusiastic mood continues in the body of the psalm, which contains the attributes or deeds of God that elicit praise.[17] Hymns include an appreciation of the universe and humanity's place within it, and express the conviction that God's presence is the social canopy under which Israel lives and worships.[18]

Reception of the Hymns

Fulgentius does not employ expressions of joy with any frequency. His community does not see itself in either temporal or spiritual circumstances in which expressions of joy or justification are appropriate. Aside from any persecution, monastic life is understood as being penitential, "white martyrdom," and the inmates of a monastery are there to purge their souls. Catharsis from the hymns falls into the penitential context and in light of the salvation of Christ. Any acknowledgement of the praise element from these psalms comes after the community has placed its needs before God.

Even though the praise element appears rarely in the collects, the hymns provide more instances for Fulgentius to perceive the presence of Christ than in other genres. He finds his inspiration in the soteriological elements of God;s active presence, and from there his christology emerges.

Mimetic Completion in the Hymns

Ps. 8:3 - *From the mouths of children and sucklings you have perfected praise.*
Collect 8 - *Perfect, Lord, the praise from the mouths of your children.*

The monks look upon themselves as children of the Lord, however, *sucklings (lactantium)* is replaced in the collect by a Pauline interpretation as a mimetic bridge. Fulgentius assumes that his monks are further along the path of spiritual perfection than the Christians at Corinth, whom Paul fed with milk, for they were not ready for solid food.[19] The monks have put off the flesh, and can accept higher spiritual challenges. We see here a rare instance of implied praise for the monks, and the successes of their spiritual disciplines.

Ps. 28:1 - *Bring to the Lord you children of God; bring to the Lord the sons of rams.*
Collect 28 - *Strip us of our evils, Lord, and grant to us contrite and humble hearts to offer in place of the sons of rams.*

In his mimetic completion of Ps. 28:1, Fulgentius evokes another psalm verse, Ps. 50:19, the contrite and humble hearts being the desired sin offerings, as rams once were in the Jerusalem Temple. The bridge for his reception appears in the Philippians hymn,[20] which connects Christ's self-emptying of pride (sin) with his sacrificial offering on the cross. The monks ask for the same purification. The Priestly addition of two verses to the end of Ps. 50 further affirms the action of emptying as preparing the way for sacrifice. Jesus's quotation of Hosea 6:6, "It is mercy I desire, not sacrifice,"[21] bring still another interpretative bridge to a richly-inspired collect.

Fulgentius here eschews the psalm's praise elements, preferring instead to teach monastic humility in the context of sacrifice.

Ps. 95:9 - *May the entire earth tremble before the face of the Lord.*
Collect 95 - *Behold . . . your entire Church, raised from earth to heaven, and made heaven itself.*

Uncharacteristically, Fulgentius changes a psalm's petition into an assertion (usually the opposite occurs), indicating Christ's fulfillment of the promise of the psalms. Salvation lifts the people of God from earthly connections. After acknowledging the Church's heavenly character, Fulgentius can confidently attack the danger of false foundations in the spiritual life caused by the deception of demons in a direct quotation from verse 5 of the psalm: *All the gods of the nations are demons, but the Lord made the heavens.* Both Lactantius and Augustine treated demonology,[22] and the psalm needs no further interpretation in order to remind the monks of infernal powers, whether they appear in their own evils forms or under the forms of heresy and persecution.

Ps. 121:7 - *May peace be in your power and abundance in your towers.*
Collect 121 - *Build the heavenly Jerusalem in us so that members might be united to members by divine grace and there might be peace in your power and abundance in your towers.*

The full revelation of the Heavenly Jerusalem[23] informs Fulgentius's reception of this Song of Ascents that contains enthusiastic praise of the city of Jerusalem. The pervasive theme allows him to address the entire psalm in the above petition, the collect's second. The *quo* clause indicates the presence of the spiritual Jerusalem in the community's practice of peace among its members, granted to them by divine grace.

Having established his reception of the entire psalm, Fulgentius offers a close paraphrase of verse 7, allowing the revelation of the psalm to speak for itself in light of the fulfillment described in the result clause. In this case, some of the joy inherent in the hymns is carried over into its collect.

Reception of Hymn Verses

Ps. 83:6-7 - *Blessed be the man whose help is in you; he placed the ascents in his heart in the valley of tears.*
Collect 83 - *From you (i.e., "with your help") our mind might ascend from the valley of weeping and bear the fruits of divine cultivation.*

Using the themes of ascent (*ascendo*) and tears (*ploratio*), Fulgentius subtly indicates a spiritual journey through penance by suggesting growth through rain, which produced the "fruits of divine cultivation."[24] There is no need for a mimetic completion here; the tears are joined to a spiritualized aspect of the monks' daily experience of cultivating crops for their food. The community has a picture of the victory of the soul (*mens*) through the action of God's grace. No further interpretation is needed, as the revelation of the psalm is complete in itself.

The Hymns and the Community's Praxis

Ps. 97:5 - *Sing to the Lord with the lyre, with the lyre and the voice of the psalm.*
Collect 97 - *In the lyre of our hearts and the voice of the psalm, we, your servants, perform our requested service asking from God the Father, so that you might save us.*

A command from the psalm is changed into an assertion that the command is being obeyed. Fulgentius addresses both the spirit and letter of the psalm by adding the song of the heart to that of the voice, indicating an awareness of Augustine's teaching on prayer in his Rule.[25] Pauline theology also offers inspiration for mimetic completion, not through literary interpretation, but through liturgical praxis. For Paul, the Israelites followed the law of the flesh and thus were able to offer fleshly praises from the voice alone.[26] The monks offer praise from their hearts and sing with the voice of the psalms in the fullness of Christ.

Ps. 98:1 - *The Lord reigns; the people grow angry.*
Collect 98 - *Perfect in us we beg, Lord, the work of your mercy, so that your people may not grow angry in your reign.*

The *ut* clause of the collect indicates the result of a petition for perfection. The liturgical praxis of the community, their *opus Dei*, is the gift of mercy.[27] Within the earlier period of revelation, the people were angry, even though the Lord reigned. As Christ's task of perfecting God's people continues, the possibility that they will become angry diminishes.

Ps. 138:12 - *For darkness will not be dark in you, and night will be illumined as day, as his darkness is, so is his light also.*
Collect 138 - *Illumine in us what is dark.*

The psalm asserts that the people's discernment of what is dark and what is light is transformed by the power of God. Fulgentius fashions the assertion into a petition for enlightenment. A spiritual rendering of the concepts of darkness and light replaces the psalm's praise elements.[28] As the community's liturgical life occurs during the darkness of Vandal persecution, compared to the darkness of the Egyptian captivity elsewhere in the collects, Fulgentius petitions God's power over the dark forces of sin and oppression that assail the monks. He calls upon God as a moral force, ignoring the joyful praise so evident in the rest of the psalm.

Ps. 145:9 - *The way of sins he destroys.*
Ps. 145:1 - *Praise the Lord, my soul.*
Collect 145 - *Destroy the way of our sins, so that our soul may always praise you in your holy temple.*

In fashioning the imperative to the soul of verse 1 into a petition, Fulgentius introduces the concept of the temple into the collect, reflecting the influence from the psalms and elsewhere in the Hebrew Scriptures.[29] The reference addresses the temporal level, indicating the room where the monks are praying, as well as the spiritual level, receiving the Pauline teaching of the body as a temple of the Holy Spirit.[30] By destroying the "way of sins," God allows the community's praxis of prayer to continue unabated, not only in the chapel where they pray, but also in their hearts wherever they may find themselves.

Soteriological Reception in the Hymns

Ps. 8:4 - *I will see your heavens: the work of your fingers.*
Ps. 8:10 - *How marvelous is your name in all the earth.*
Collect 8 - *Save us, we beg, the works of your fingers, so that your name may be marvelous among the human race all over the earth.*

The *ut* clause, indicating a mimetic completion, depicts a result of the act of salvation, which appears as a straightforward proclamation in the psalm. Fulgentius shifts the psalmist's awe in the face of creation into a soteriological context, acknowledging the continuing salvific action of God.

Significantly, Fulgentius does not interpret verses 5-8, which include Israel's wonder that the position of humankind is "little less than the angels,"[31] and thus eschews a possible cathartic bridge, the central position of verses 5-8 in the Letter to the Hebrews.[32] Instead, there is a theological statement of total dependence on the Lord. Grace allows the community to experience the centrality of salvation through Jesus Christ. Even as they acknowledge their place in creation (*the works of your fingers*), the community begs for salvation from the source of their existence.

Christ in the Hymns

Ps. 32:1 - *Exult (you) just in the Lord; praise from the upright is fitting.*
Collect 32 - *Although we are not just, it is nevertheless just for us to rejoice in you Lord almighty God.*

The dramatic imperative from the beginning of the psalm brings forth a mimetic completion based on the doctrine of justification. No one is just except Christ, who *is* justice. His presence and grace allow people to exult, and thus fulfill the psalm's injunction in a way the Israelites could not. The cathartic bridge comes from the Epistle to the Romans, which teaches that the Christian rejects justification through his or her actions, a concept that characterizes the Israelite community for Paul, in favor of justification through Christ.[33] The beginning of the collect affirms this teaching with its claim that no one is just. Even though the Father is the only *prosopon* addressed in this collect, the community realizes that they may fully rejoice in the Father only through the justification of Christ.

Ps. 86:1 - *His foundation is on the holy mountain.*
Ps. 86:5 - *This one and that one were born in her.*
Collect 86 - *Perfect the foundation of the feet of our soul. Place them on the holy mountains, so that, in him who as our God on earth was made human, you may allow us to abide through infinite ages, so that he himself may abide in us who with you lives and reigns as God in unity with the Holy Spirit through all ages.*[34]

The simplicity of Christological expression near the beginning of the collect excerpt avoids the complexities of the christological controversies that receive attention in other collects. Both Jesus's identity as a Jew (being born in her, i.e., Sion; see Ps. 86:2) and credal statements from the early Church[35] inform Fulgentius in his composition. The *ut* clause introduces an eschatological petition not taken from the psalm text, expressing the desire for eternal life and happiness, and the collect ends with a Trinitarian formula that complements the simplicity of the earlier christological statement.

Ps. 97:5 - *Sing to the Lord in the lyre, in the lyre and the voice of the psalm.*
Ps. 97:1b - *He will save with his right hand and his holy arm.*
Ps. 97:2b - *In the sight of the nations he has revealed his justice.*
Collect 97 (complete) - *In the lyre of our hearts and the voice of the psalm, we, your servants, perform our required service to you so that you may save us by your right hand and your strong arm and in Christ your salvation, now manifested to all the nations.*

In collect 32, we saw that the personification of Christ as justice informed Fulgentius's interpretation. Here, God's justice, addressed in verse 2b, is received as God's instrument of salvation: Christ. The community's liturgical praxis becomes linked to salvation in the beginning of the collect. After having affirmed that the community continues to perform its "required service," the Opus Dei, the collect leads to expressions of confidence in God's power and salvation. Christ's salvation is connected to the theme of God's powerful limbs from verse 1, and, as the community of the psalmist perceives the universal expression of God's power, so does the monastic community see the universality of Christ's salvation.

Psalm 110:1-2a - *I confess to you, Lord, with my whole heart in the council of the just and the great works of the Lord.*
Ps. 110:8 - *. . . made in truth and justice.*
Ps. 110:9 - *He has sent redemption to his people.*
Collect 110 (complete) - *Grant us, Lord, to praise your works in the council and congregation of the just, works done in truth and justice, so that you may preserve the redeemed in the Redeemer and may grant pardon to your people.*

The psalm offers effusive praise to God, but the collect declares that the praise has a proper context, that of truth and justice, with specific results listed in the *quo* clause.

The term, "congregation of the just" (*consilio rectorum*), allows for some speculation on the term *rector*. Fourth century usage renders the term as "bishop,"[36] thus offering a possible double interpretation. On one level, the righteous people are the monks who praise God within the context of the Office. The other context referring to bishops relates the contexts of God's works to the entire Church, including the

Church's proper governance. The "councils" can refer to the monastic community meetings, as well as prayer sessions, but also to local councils of bishops, both those secret meetings at home and those held in exile, as well as the Ecumenical Councils, from where much collect material comes.

The Collects for the Royal Psalms

Scholars designate psalms as "royal" or "Messianic" due to their content rather than to literary form. Any psalm that includes in its setting experiences from the life of the king receives that designation.[37]

The *Sitz im Leben* of Israel's king described by the psalms and their titles does not appear in the collects,[38] But Fulgentius does respond to the royal theme. Predictably, the kingship of Christ[39] forms the basis of his interpretations of the royal psalms. He also uses them to teach orthodox Christology[40] and New Testament themes.[41] Fulgentius seems to have classified this genre similarly to modern form criticism.

Mimetic Completion in the Royal Psalms

Ps. 44:11 - *Forget your people and your father's house.*
Ps. 44:13 - *The wealthy among the people entreat your countenance.*
Ps. 44:3 - *Beautiful in form compared to the sons of men.*
Ps. 44:5 - . . . *by your comeliness and beauty; continue, prosper, so formed, and reign according to truth and gentleness and justice.*
Collect 44 (complete) - *All the wealthy of the people have forgotten their nation and their father's house, God almighty Father. We, your sons, have pursued comeliness and beauty; therefore, hear us and prosper us so that we may always be pleasing in your eyes.*

The verses chosen for the collect's first sentence concern the advice given to the king's bride before the royal wedding. Fulgentius subtly interprets the royal aspects of the psalm outside of the *Sitz im Leben* of the addressee. He employs a cathartic bridge, taken from the Gospel admonition concerning the potential for the rich to enter into the kingdom of heaven.[42] The bridge allows him to treat one of the few psalm references to the wealthy in order to affirm the life of poverty followed by his monks, and highlight its subsequent reward.

The collect's second sentence takes the royal flattery of verses 3 and 5 and fashions them into a petition. The term, "sons of men" indicates the superiority of the king's attractiveness over that of other men.

Another cathartic bridge comes from Jesus's self-identification as the "Son of Man," throughout the Gospels. As King of Heaven he is above all other in spiritual comeliness. The monks' pursuance of spiritual beauty indicates an element of *imitatio Christi* in the collect. The catharsis for the monks centers upon the comparison of their true king, Christ, to an earthly king, who in this case is an Arian Vandal. Any flattery to such a one as he would be out of the question!

The Royal Psalms and the Community's Praxis

> Ps. 100:2 - *I will discern the immaculate way when you will come to me; I was walking in the innocence of my heart in the midst of my house.*
> Ps. 100:7 - *He who speaks evil has not acted rightly in the sight of my eyes.*
> Collect 100 (complete) - *Remove the evil object from our eyes, Lord, and cause us to walk in the midst of your house in our innocence. Take away pride which we admit is the beginning of transgression, so that our whole man may serve you in the immaculate way.*

Modern criticism interprets Psalm 100 as a liturgical expression of oaths taken by the king, either at his coronation of at a festival commemorating a coronation.[43] Its collect contains a depiction of the voice of Christ in the psalms, one of the themes upon which Augustine bases his exegesis. "My house" of verse 2 becomes "your house" in the collect, thus identifying the true owner of the house. The second sentence indicates that Fulgentius is doing a bit of "goal setting" for the monks, asking for the removal of pride during prayer, and certainly in their daily relationships with each other.

The hermeneutic of the collect binds the community's utterance of the psalm to the promises in the text of the collect. The praxis of their speech allows for an interpretation that brings their understanding of the psalm more fully into the light of Christ's revelation. Christians cannot act for good without the help of God, so the psalm leads Fulgentius to bring the contents of the psalm into proper Christian systems of address and petition. The collect offers a "second opinion" to the liturgical praxis, and increases the community's mandate to act justly within the action of their prayer.[44]

> Ps. 131:5 - . . . *until I find a place for the Lord, a tabernacle for the God of Jacob.*
> Collect 131 - *Grant us Lord, we beg, to find a place for you, the Lord, to prepare a place for you in our hearts.*

Psalm 131 begins with King David's oath not to build a palace for himself until he builds a house for the Lord, an incident found nowhere else in the Hebrew Scriptures.

Fulgentius shifts the object of the oath from David's promised house to a petition that the Lord build a spiritual temple for them, a center for the preparation of their hearts. The identity of the temple shifts also, from a place where animals served as sin offerings to the monastery, a place for spiritual sacrifices, which exists solely due to the work of the Lord. Christ's revelation subjugates human kingship to divine rule, certainly a reminder to the monks of the Vandal kings, who still reigned through the cult of personality. Far from denying Davidic kingship, the community affirms its continuance in the person of Christ.

Soteriological Interpretation in the Royal Psalms

Ps. 2:2 - *The kings of the earth make a stand and rulers assemble as one against the Lord and against his anointed.*
Collect 2 (complete) - *May you never permit the most evil demon to go through our lands, for the entire passion of human substance fell by lot to Christ while he was providing himself with it in the Virgin. Therefore grant us, we beg, to live on in him of whom we are all members in part, so that serving you, God and Father, in fear, we may deserve to obtain the rewards of blessedness.*

For this community, there is no doubting the true royal identity of the Lord's anointed, with the kings and rulers of the earth, especially the Vandal kings, being interpreted as agents of "the evil demon." The phrase, "our lands" (*nostrae terrae*), could indicate the province of Byzacena, which had been overrun by the "demon" Vandals, or the lands of the monastery itself. The petition is connected to the victory of Christ's passion, and is further attached to a remarkable expression and interpretation of the doctrine of the *Theotokos* from the Council of Ephesus (431), which affirmed Mary as the Mother of God. Fulgentius, possibly approached by his monks to clarify the teaching, came up with this wonderful phrasing affirming the divine and human elements of the Incarnation.

The petition of the collect's second sentence indicates an interpretation taken from Paul's theology of the body[45] and of the Church,[46] and continues the theme from the previous sentence. Christ's human and divine natures defeated Satan, and they continue to exist in Christ's body, the Church.

Collect 2 affirms the community's identity in a perilous world, employing scrupulously orthodox Incarnation theology. Its mode of expression further highlights Fulgentius's theological and literary talents.

> Ps. 109:1-2 - *The Lord said to my lord, 'Sit at my right hand, until I place your enemies at your footstool.' The Lord will send forth the staff of your virtue, to rule in the midst of your enemies.*
> Collect 109 (complete) - *In the midst of our enemies, Lord, make us to dominate, so that we, who have already merited to sit at your right hand in Christ, your Son, our creator and Lord, may merit to possess the eternal fatherland with all the saints.*

Although the temporal prerogative of the victorious king of Israel, military and regal power, holds no interest for Fulgentius, he uses the images of the psalm to address a more important concern: realized eschatology. In Christ's victory over sin and death, Christians have already received a place at God;s right hand as members of Christ's body. The oracle of the psalm no longer predicts the future, but asserts the achieved salvation of Christ.

Christ as creator is consonant with Catholic interpretation of John 1:1-3. The words of the psalm itself serve to proclaim Christ's relationship to the Father, the coeternal existence of the *logos*.[47] Even though Christ's role as creator forms part of the Arian belief system,[48] the collect petition to possess the *eternal* fatherland implies that relationship of Father and Son that the Arians had rejected.

> Ps. 71:12 - *He has freed the poor from the powerful man.*
> Ps. 71:13 - *He will save the souls of the poor.*
> Collect 71 (complete) - *Do not despise the souls of your poor, Lord; let that one rescue us from the hand of the powerful one about whom the prophets sang; and may he rule from sea to sea is us, Jesus Christ our God who with you lives and reigns.*

The community here identifies itself with the poor who depend upon the justice of the king. Even though the collect does not specifically identify the power that enslaves the poor, verses 4 and 9 of the psalm aid in this with their references to *calumniatorum* and *inimici*. These terms, the second of which appears several times in the collects, together with the collect's closing petition that affirms the unity and shared divinity of Father and Son, identify the *inimici* as Arian heretics. Fulgentius is once again subtle in his identification of enemies, employing a mixture of political language taken from the psalm, and theological language to interpret the psalm's christological message and affirm the community's beliefs and sufferings.

The Collects for the Wisdom Psalms

As is the case with the Royal Psalms, Wisdom Psalms are classified by content rather than by literary form.[49] Both the Hebrew Scriptures and Rabbinic writings personify and extol Wisdom.[50] Those psalms that contain wisdom material address a desirable characteristic or guiding force rather than a personified entity.

The Wisdom Psalms evoke a closer reception of mood from Fulgentius than other psalm genres. Verses chosen from these psalms generally receive an interpretation consonant with Christian wisdom teaching. Wisdom leads to action, and the psalms provide the community with the proper attitudes for their praxis. Collects for the Wisdom Psalms virtually repeat the theology of the psalms themselves, and require little further interpretation, and are more positive in overall mood than collects related to other genres.

Wisdom Psalms and the Community's Praxis

Ps. 1:1-2 - *Blessed the man who...will meditate on [the Lord's] law day and night.*
Collect 1 - *Visit us in your salvation, Lord, so that we may meditate continually upon your law day and night.*

Fulgentius receives the psalm in the context of the monastic prayer schedule, which exists through God's grace, the sole source of their blessedness. As the psalter opens with an unambiguous delineation of good and evil,[51] so the collects begin with an affirmation of the community's search for wisdom.

Ps. 33:14 - *Keep your tongue from evil.*
Ps. 33:2 - *His praise is always in my mouth.*
Ps. 33:15 - *Seek peace.*
Ps. 33:16 - *The eyes of the Lord are upon them and his ears are attentive to their prayers.*
Collect 33 (complete) - *Restrain our tongue from evil, Lord, so that your praise may always be in our mouth. Grant, we beg, to your people to seek and to follow your peace, so that you might watch over us with your eyes and your ears may be attentive to our prayers.*

Fulgentius brings together three verses from a segment of Ps. 33 that presents a series of admonitions from parent to child. Within its liturgical praxis, the community prays that its communal relationships may reflect its worship. Grace keeps one's tongue from evil so that it may do its proper work of praise. God's vigilance is a comfort in the psalm; in the collect, it has a distinct objective, to oversee the prayers of the community. Fulgentius does not place the community among the just, as does the psalm, Christian spirituality precludes that, but he attributes all good things to grace.

Spiritual Interpretation of the Wisdom Psalms

Ps. 1:3 - *He will be like a tree . . . that will yield its fruit in due time.*
Collect 1 - *. . . so that we may return to you the fruits of divine cultivation in their time.*

The *ut* clause here follows a petition which has been partially erased in the manuscript; the remaining words request: *build us . . . through your grace.* Fulgentius brings the theme of bearing fruit directly into Christian wisdom, evoking God as vinegrower,[52] thus connecting the agricultural employment of the monks to their spiritual growth. By giving themselves over to God's own time, the collect follows the train of wisdom thought in giving up autonomous desires to the grace of God.

The Collects for the Exodus Psalms

Themes of the Exodus appear in psalms that belong to several of Gunkel's categories.[53] Fulgentius consistently addresses the Exodus themes in those psalms that contain them, employing those verses that refer to God's leading the Israelites out of Egypt,[54] the columns of fire and cloud,[55] the episode of Dathan and Abiron,[56] and the "spirit of Pharaoh."[57] Psalm 19 is not an Exodus psalm, but its reference to chariots and horses provides a context for Fulgentius to make an Exodus interpretation.

This strength of interpretation indicates that Fulgentius went through a process of genre identification. God's salvific acts for the Israelites in the face of extermination by an implacable enemy engages Fulgentius more intensely than other psalm themes. He receives those acts as pertinent to the situation of his community. His classification calls forth a spiritualized interpretation that evokes dependence upon grace. The collects portray the continuance of salvation that began in the Exodus, and has reached its fulfillment in the redemption of Christ.

Exodus Psalms mark the primal moment of Israel's relationship with God, focused from its origin on Israel's liturgical life in the Passover Ritual. The monastic community uses the collects as a cathartic bridge to affirm the promise of a moment of liberation for the new Israel.[58]

Fulgentius's treatment of the Exodus psalms reflects the religio-political references made in sermons of the period and in Victor of Vita's *Historia persecutionis*. His use of the Exodus themes indicate that he followed a mode of commentary in which figures from biblical history posed as surrogates for contemporary tyrants. He is thus able to address Vandal occupation through the context of Christian prayer.

The Flight From Egypt

Ps. 80:10-11 - *No newcomer god will be among you, nor shall you adore an alien god; indeed I am the Lord your God, who led you out of Egypt.*
Collect 80 - *Do not surrender us into the hand of the enemy, the devil, because you, Lord, are our God who led us out of the land of Egypt.*

The Exodus connection exploited by Fulgentius in this collect also appears in the Decalogue.[59] By characterizing the enemies as diabolical, Fulgentius spiritualizes the experience of the community in its battle against Satan. He also heaps more scorn upon the head of the community's temporal enemies and their heresy. The tone recalls the "reminder" portion of the Lament Psalms, in which Israel lists God's previous salvific acts with the purpose of indicating that such help us needed once again. Instead of the phrase of command from the Decalogue, Fulgentius shifts the emphasis to reminder, implying that the community keeps the commandment and needs deliverance from those who do not.

Ps. 104:37 - *He led them out in silver and gold.*
Ps. 104:39 - *He spread a cloud for their protection, and fire, so that it might shine for them through the night.*
Collect 104 - *Lead us out of the darkness of this Egypt, so that there may be no weakling in our tabernacle. Spread the cloud in our protection until we may take the eternal fatherland.*

Fulgentius's reference to "this Egypt" suggests several possible interpretations. Egypt signifies slavery to sin, as well as the political subjection experienced by the monks. Either, or preferable, both, form the subject of the reference. The *ut* clause refers to weakness, and indicates a malady of a political or spiritual, as opposed to physical, nature. Who is the "weakling?" Certainly he is one who did not have the spiritual strength to face the particular demands of monastic life at this difficult historical period. Such a one may be present in the monastery, but is rejected from the tabernacle, the place of prayer, which would indicate the community's "heart." For their prayer to be efficacious, the spiritual strength of every monk is needed. The final goal of the prayer is the taking of the "eternal fatherland." The verb *capio* indicates military seizure, but in this case the victory is won through spiritual means. The monks must match the temporal rapaciousness of the Vandals through prayer, and thus wrest heaven from the hands of the heretics.

Ps. 113:1 - . . . *in Israel's exit from Egypt.*
Ps. 113:12 - *The images of the nations are silver and gold, the works of the hands of men.*
Collect 113 - *Lord, restorer of human nature who, through your gratuitous gift, freed from the dark death of Egypt and from the idols of the nations, the works of the hands of men, transferred us into the kingdom of the light of your Son.*

Fulgentius concentrates on the pain endured by the Israelites during the Egyptian period, and includes another echo of the "reminder" portion of the lament genre. Through grace, God not only led the people out of Egypt and physical peril, but also out of the spiritual peril of idolatry. Salvation here is realized, as the collect states that the same action of grace, the gratuitous gift, has already brought the monks out of the peril of an unholy christology. By addressing the important themes of light and darkness, Fulgentius clearly indicates the "way" into which his community has been led.

The Columns of Fire and Cloud

Collect 77 (complete)[60] - *The miracles which you worked for our fathers are not hidden, God, omnipotent Father; you fed them with your manna and gave them water to drink from the spiritual rock that carried the figure of Christ. Lead us too, Lord, in a column of cloud through the day and a column of fire through the night, until we cross over the sea of this world, and deserve to possess the land of the living through your grace.*

The two columns only begin to indicate the richness of inspiration supplied by the Exodus theme in this collect, which also includes Israel's Sinai experience. The interpretation of the *petra spiritalis* as Christ comes from Paul.[61] In addition, Fulgentius evokes the Living

Waters of the fourth Gospel,[62] in the context of eschatological fulfillment.

An allegory appears in the interpretation of the Red Sea. It represents the dangers of this world, through which we are guided by God's presence. Instead of the columns guiding Israel to the sea, from where the Lord then deals with Pharaoh's army,[63] the columns lead through the temptations of the world and into the heavenly kingdom.

By invoking the column of cloud, Fulgentius shifts the interpretation of the psalmist, who refers to the cloud that covered the dwelling tent.[64] Fulgentius's shift highlights the protective actions of God against a pursuing army (the Vandals?) within the public context of community prayers.

Another feature of this collect is the interpretation of the rock in allegorical terms more suitable to a treatise than to a prayer. Fulgentius indulges in the occasional exegetical explanation, using it to teach his monks, offering the exegesis as an aid to their meditation.

Ps. 134:7 - *Leading out clouds from the end of the earth, he turned lightning into rain.*
Collect 134 - *Raise in us the clouds of apostolic teaching.*

Even though the Exodus references in Ps. 134 are limited to a brief mention of the plagues, the cloud imagery, used by the psalmist in a meteorological sense, brings out a spiritual interpretation from Fulgentius. Certainly the verb, *educo* (to lead), evokes the Exodus in a way that Fulgentius uses in collect 77, while the verb *suscito* can indicate the raising of a structure (a pillar), as well as resurrection in the Christian usage of the time. For Fulgentius, the protective and guiding action of the cloud continues into the Christian era. As the cloud led Israel out of Egypt and into the Sinai encounter, so did the *kerygma* of the Apostles lead the Church into her ongoing encounter with Christ.

Dathan and Abiron

Ps. 105:17 - *The earth opened and swallowed Dathan, and covered the association of Abiron.*
Collect 105 - *Save your people from the perdition of Dathan and Abiron and those like them.*

The psalm evokes an episode from Israel's Sinai experience[65] during which Dathan and Abiron (Abiram), forming an insurrection against Moses, are destroyed in the manner described above. The incident inspires Fulgentius to his only fantastic composition among the collects. Usually immediate and realistic in his interpretations, he here appeals to a punishing action of God that exhibits divine anger in a manner unprecedented in the collects. However, Dathan and Abiron are schismatics,[66] and when one applies the image of being swallowed by the earth to the placing of Hell (*she'ol* in Num. 16:33 and in the psalms, but interpreted similarly to Hell by Christians in Late Antiquity), then the true spiritual fate of the two becomes clear. By abandoning his usual restraint, Fulgentius offers a strong cathartic bridge for his monks and communicates clearly both the oppression that the community endures from the Arian Vandals, and the eternal punishment awaiting those same oppressors.

Pharaoh

Ps. 19:8 - *These on chariots and these on horses, however, we will call on the name of the Lord our God.*
Collect 19 - *Protect us from all evil, so that the spiritual Pharaoh may come to ruin in horses and chariots as we rise up.*

Identified as a royal psalm in Gunkel's form-critical model, Fulgentius includes this in his genre of Exodus psalms. The mention of chariots and horses evokes the theme, and points to the possibility of Fulgentius's use of political criticism. Victor of Vita reports the use of code names in sermons of the time that stood in for the Vandal kings,[67] with figures such as Pharaoh, Nebuchadnezzer, Herod, and Holofernes standing in for the Vandal kings.[68] Fulgentius shows himself capable of such tactics that could not help but to allow his monks some sort of cathartic expression within a frustrating and dangerous living situation.

Even though there is no overt interpretation of verse 7 in the collect,[69] the theme of God's Anointed and the strength of God's right arm that it contains informs the collect interpretation of verse 8. The monks can "rise up" only through the strength of Christ, which will vanquish the strength of the spirit of Pharaoh, which lives on in the Vandal kingdom. The kingdom of heaven will overcome the earthly one that persecutes God's people.

Ps. 135:15 - *He overthrew Pharaoh and his power in the Red Sea.*
Collect 135 - *Lord, look upon the affliction of your people, long troubled . . . so that, when the spiritual Pharaoh has been conquered and we have obtained the land of our people as an inheritance, we may all say in our humility: May the Lord be mindful of us.*

Fulgentius interprets verse 15 of the psalm in the manner of the "reminder" portion of the Lament genre, and Pharaoh's demise provides the interpretation with another theme for addressing the Vandal occupation. The petition for the return of the land was not to be fulfilled until 525, when Byzantine forces under Belisarius put an end to Vandal rule.

Much care went into the composition of this collect. The plea for liberation occurs in the psalmic context of enslavement in Egypt and Israel's eventual domination of Canaan. The inherited land does not seem to be spiritualized, as one would expect, but appears in the context of hope that the Lord will provide a political reward for all of the suffering the people have endured. The petition is a frank plea for relief.

The Collects for the Penitential Psalms

The seven Penitential Psalms[70] form the oldest known collection of psalms used for a particular purpose by Christians. They have been singled out throughout the history of interpretation as providing a spiritual journey of penitence. Gunkel places them into a sub-genre of the lament psalms.[71]

Possidius, Augustine's biographer, provides the earliest known example of the use of psalms as a vehicle for penitential prayer, as well as an early example of the creation of psalm genres. According to his account, Augustine prayed certain "psalms of David" on his deathbed as a form of penitence.[72] A study by Dr. Harry Nasuti of Fordham University has posited that Augustine used the seven psalms that later became identified as penitential.[73] His review of Augustine's theology, especially the interpretation of Paul's Letter to the Romans, and the anti-Pelagian works, has led Nasuti to make a stronger Augustinian connection to the tradition than that offered by Possidius's work alone.

The earliest sure identification of the genre was by Cassiodorus,[74] who did not identify the source of his classification. In between the periods of Possidius and Cassiodorus, Fulgentius wrote his psalm orations. Investigation of the collects for the seven psalms indicate that he knew of the genre, and his proximity to Augustine, as well as his reception of Augustinian theology, offer some further evidence that Augustine was the first to collect these particular psalms into a genre.

Reception of the Penitential Psalms

Fulgentius's collects for the seven psalms refer to sin, wrath, punishment, forgiveness, and healing in a manner that one might expect given the penitential nature of monastic life. Even the collects for those Penitential Psalms that do not specifically mention sin[75] contain expressions of penitence. None of the collects refers to specific sins or punishments, which is in keeping with Fulgentius's practice of keeping specifics out of the compositions. He thus allowed each monk to meditate on his personal sinfulness, need for punishment or forgiveness, and relationship with God.

While other collects contain terms for sin identical with those used in the penitential collects,[76] the tone of those psalms that these other collects accompany evokes the comforting grace of God. Their collects address community concerns such as orthodoxy and heresy, gratuitous grace, the Vandal, occupation and entry into eternal life. In the penitential collects the theme of penitence overshadows all of these other topics. Taken in order, they form a spiritual pilgrimage through the acts and emotions of the penitent. Collect 6 contains expressions of total surrender to the comprehension of personal sinfulness. The five subsequent collects treat various aspects of sin and punishment: deliverance from anxiety, escape from god's wrath, rejection by God, eternal death, and God's attention to entreaty. The petitions in these middle collects, especially in collect 31, ask in no uncertain terms for deliverance from punishment. Collect 142 acts as a closing expression of penitence and interprets the theme of justification in a Pauline manner that helps to focus the thoughts of the penitent on his final desire: salvation.

Fulgentius's reliance on Augustinian theology in the orations, especially his anti-Pelagian stance, supports the position that he interpreted these seven psalms as penitential because of Augustine's usage and identification. In addition to other aspects of Augustinian theology, Fulgentius employs terms and themes from the Letter to the Romans in the collects.

Penitential Themes

Sin

Six of the seven collects refer explicitly to sin. Collects 6 and 31, the first two of the series, contain acknowledgement of sin, the first step for the penitent. The former offers a larger view by acknowledging the "weakness of our nation" before its confession of sinful acts. Collect 31 recognizes both sin and injustice, and its bold declaration of sinfulness leads the soul on its way to salvation and forgiveness.

Further on in the seven, Fulgentius examines the concept of sinfulness more closely, and variations occur. Collect 37 refers to "illusions," which assault even those who live the monastic life. Acknowledging this power enables the penitent to appeal to God's mercy.

Collect 50 includes "our injustice"[77] as its sin reference. Having the declaration of sin already present in the psalm,[78] Fulgentius concentrates on interpreting the concepts of sin and injustice in the sight of God's justice.

Psalm 101 presents thematic problems, as nowhere is there any conventional penitential expressions, only a reference in verse 11 to God's wrath. Fulgentius's use of verse 21[79] in his interpretation acknowledges that the human tendency towards sin began with the first couple and continues in all people.[80]

The Wrath of God

The petitions for deliverance from the manifestations of God's anger found in the seven psalms appear in close proximity to acknowledgement of sinfulness in the penitential collects.

Collect 37 closely interprets the beginning of the psalm.[81] The arrows afflicting the lamenter are products of God's wrath, which both psalmist and monks recognize as intolerable, though temporary, sufferings. The collect expresses both confidence and hope that its petition for removal of the arrows will be heard. The community of monks declares that its realization that illusions cause sin will in turn cause God to withhold a more final, permanent act of wrath.[82]

This ultimate expression of God's wrath, the fear of vanishing into nothingness, also appears in Ps. 101.[83] The collect addresses this fear from the viewpoint of realized redemption, and does not consider that such punishment will be a reality for anyone who adores God. Fulgentius's interpretation of the collect as part of the penitential tradition is subtle, as is the penitential aspect of the psalm itself, and points to the existence of a body of penitential psalms known to the author that included the puzzling Ps. 101.

Healing

In their requests for healing, collects 6 and 37 offer interpretations that follow the psalm texts closely.[84] Ps. 6:3 requires spiritual interpretation in order to remind the community that sin placed their souls in jeopardy. Ps. 37:4 places the complaint in proximity to an acknowledgement of sinfulness. The psalmist's expression of penitential motivation enables the author to employ the verse more literally in order to remind the community of the penitential aspects of the psalm.

Redemption, Forgiveness, and Salvation

Various treatments of soteriological themes, containing a mixture of petition and confidence, appear in three collects. Collects 31 and 129 ask for redemption, a petition shared with five other collects in the *Africana* series.[85] Both collects place their petitions for redemption near an acknowledgement of sin.[86] The request of collect 129 begins with local confession and proceeds to intercede for the whole Church in the person of the Chosen People. The extraordinary demand for pardon expressed in collect 31 (*you, pardon us*, admittedly more forceful in English translation than in the original Latin), resembles the demands for help and the "certainty of a hearing" portions of the lament genre.[87]

Collect 142 connects salvation to rescue through the medium of divine grace, and connects it to the action of "your good Spirit," as it leads the monks into the "right way."

Collect 142: A Closing for the Seven

Collect 142's expressions of hastening to make satisfaction serves to continue rather than conclude the urgent journey of the penitent, and connects this collect with the concept of a reward for true penitence in collect 6. Through penitential activity, the sinner indicates readiness for the reception of grace and forgiveness.

The judgment theme of Ps. 142:2,[88] and the intent of following in the *uia recta*, symbolize future avoidance of sin through the acceptance of the Law.

Collect 142's themes come from an identification with a penitential tradition rather than from the psalm text itself. The journey of the penitent both quickens and continues in a circle with this last penitential collect, further heightened by the allusion to the grace theme of collect 6.

Fulgentius's interpretation of these seven psalms are expressions of his overriding concern: the spiritual welfare of his community. His task of guiding souls to God forms seven psalms into a spiritual journey of penitence. In the liturgical setting, the monks experience penitence through communal prayer and personal meditation, aided by the psalms and their collects.

Summary

Fulgentius received the psalms as revealed texts. The imperfect revelation of the pre-Christian era offered him the opportunity to interpret chosen portions of psalm texts in a personal manner, always with Christ in mind. By either consciously or unconsciously employing critical techniques appropriated from classical paradigms, he shifted the methods of interpretation that others had used before him, as the extended theological treatise was impractical in a liturgical setting. The shift results in orations of intense inspiration that applied scriptural texts to the daily spiritual and temporal concerns of a North African monastic community.

Through the course of composing his orations, Fulgentius showed recognition of psalm genres. His interpretation of certain psalms coincided with the genre that Gunkel later identified as "wisdom" psalms. He composed within the bounds of the lament tradition, and created a genre of his own from Exodus themes. Finally, he received the newer genre classification of Penitential Psalms, possibly from Augustine himself.

Fulgentius's ingenuity and literary flair resulted in flexible interpretations that emerged from a regular exposure to the texts within the milieu of his monastic community. Only after having lived with the psalms for such an extended period could such interpretations have emerged.

CHAPTER 4

North African Theology and Rhetoric in the Collects

Fulgentius of Ruspe was a theologian and a teacher. His frequent repetition in the collects of his numerous theological convictions emerge from his desire to instruct all of the members of his community, especially the recalcitrant.[1] His insistence upon teaching orthodox theology attests to the fact that he lived in a theologically beleaguered age.

His position as abbot and his literary abilities[2] resulted in individuality of phrasing and theological expression, so individual as to share relatively few technical terms with his theological "mentor," Augustine. Such expressive independence further indicates a rhetorical technique that, limited though it is within the collect genre, exploits that genre's limitations in order to present a digest of the thoughts of councillor documents and theological treatises for his monks to ponder. The abruptness itself is a rhetorical technique, using the authority of the liturgy as the main platform for teaching.

Fulgentius's originality and choice of verses for interpretation place him slightly apart from other authors in the tradition of Latin psalm interpretation. However, his reception of orthodox theology represents the North African mainstream, especially as embodied in Augustine's writings. Brou's suggestion of Ferrandus, Facundus, Verecundus and Fulgentius as possible authors indicates the theological connection of all four to each other and to Augustine.

In addition to Augustinian orthodoxy, Fulgentius affirms the teachings of the christological "Definition" of Chalcedon in several collects. In addition to Verecundus's excerpts from Chalcedon, which merely touch upon canons that deal with orthodox christology,[3] fuller treatments of the subject appear in North African writers such as Vigilius of Thapsis,[4] and Liberatus, deacon of Carthage,[5] as well as Fulgentius's own treatises. Emperor Justinian's clumsy attempt at reconciliation with the non-Chalcedonians, the condemnation of the

Three Chapters,[6] drew opposition from Pontianus of Ignota[7] as well as Facundus and Verecundus.[8]

Fulgentius, who debated king Thrasamund on christological topics, earns his place within the combative North African tradition. The royal encounter, his treatises and the testimony of Ferrandus's *Vita* place him firmly into the orthodox tradition. The collects' intimate venue of composition and usage indicate that the theological issues of the day were not solely the provenance of public debate and discourses but were also material for monastic teaching and meditation.

Augustinian Grace Theology and the Collects

The two aspects of Augustine's thought that most influenced Fulgentius were his theology of grace and the anti-Pelagian writings. In addition to the specially-chosen psalm verses, Fulgentius incorporated a good deal of grace theology into the orations, teaching both the orthodox position on the topic and encouraging the monks to pray for various kinds of grace to aid them in their lives.

In the collects, Fulgentius not only received contemporary theological thought, but uses the liturgy to disseminate it into the community. Repeated praying of the psalms and their collects formed a rhetorical device in itself, and the monks could comprehend the all-important role of grace in their lives within the framework of Augustine's thought.

The Workings of Grace

Forty-eight collects refer to aspects of God's grace in such terms as *gratia*,[9] *munus*[10] and *misericordia*. These references include modifiers such as *tua*,[12] *diuina*,[13] and the important Augustinian term, *gratuita*.[14] Twice, the collects make reference to *totum gratie quod rogamus*.[15]

As the above list suggests, Fulgentius took advantage of the richness of grace theology as envisioned by Augustine. For Augustine, grace is the necessary gift that counteracts the effects of Original Sin, and allows the individual to resist temptation. The created soul has no instability; its capacity for understanding truth provides hope for the attainment of the spiritual realm, with the resulting bonus of living a good life on earth. This good life, the life of grace, brings the soul to the point of desiring only that which can be possessed by will and cannot be lost unwillingly, that is, freedom from the desires of the body. Under grace, such freedom can be sought by the individual soul.[16]

According to Augustine, the Church is the place where the search for grace receives its fullest expression. Schismatics and heretics cannot experience grace, nor can anyone else, no matter how well-intentioned, experience the grace of salvation without first having been baptized into the Church.[17] Outside the Church, people cannot live the full life of the Spirit, cannot keep God's Law, and are therefore doomed.

God's Law cannot be kept by the individual alone, as it falls beyond human capability, and this impossibility is itself God's preparation for individual humility, and eventually, faith. Faith and grace are gifts that keep one from falling into despair at the impossibility of living the moral life on one's own. These gifts are gratuitous as people do nothing to deserve them, but all the good they do flows from them.[18]

In the *Enarrationes in Psalmos*, and elsewhere,[19] Augustine identifies the psalms as the prayer of Christ, and they represent for him the journey towards salvation. He differentiated among various types of grace in his works: protective, salvific, forgiving, frequent, and eschatological. Fulgentius is aware of such differentiation, and this awareness appears in the collects.

Among the reasons for teaching his monks about grace was the need to combat Pelagianism, and, possibly the need to avoid misinterpretation of Augustine's grace theology that occurred during his lifetime, especially from the monastery at Hadrumetum. Part of his rhetorical technique was the use of the rich terminology of grace, and its appearance in so many collects indicates its importance to the spiritual life of Fulgentius and his monks.

Protective Grace

Ps. 15:1 - *Keep me Lord, for I hope in you.*
Collect 15 - *Therefore, keep us by your gratuitous grace.*
Collect 96 - *Protect, Lord, by your gratuitous grace . . . that, hating evil, we may love you, Lord out God.*
Collect 118.6 (complete) - *Lord, defender of our souls, allot to us to love your law, and to have hatred for our enemies, so you do not confuse us from our hopes, but protect us through your gratuitous grace.*

God's protective power had great value for a monastery under theological, political and, possibly, military siege. Collect 15 receives the text of its psalm by using *conserua nos* in its petition for grace. All three collects use the term *gratuita*, teaching that those who did indeed receive such grace have received it through no action of their own.

The moral declaration of Ps. 96:10 appears in the collect as an affirmation of grace. The above petition opens the collect, and does not interpret a psalm verse. Its resulting *quo* close, which comes at the end of the collect, makes the connection with the psalm verse.[20] Fulgentius identifies a two-way action: God loves those who hate evil; those who hate evil, by definition, love God, and live under the protection of the grace which causes them to love.

Collect 118.6 is an adaptation of the entire text of section (*he*) of the psalm, which contains the elements of hatred for evildoers and petitions for God's help. The proper choice of sides, made by the working of protective grace, results in fulfilled hopes. God's role as protector of the faithful includes illuminating them in their decision between good and evil.

Fulgentius interprets the Augustinian stages of the life of grace in an intense, personal manner.[21] The second of the four stages: acceptance of life under the Law, signifies the Mosaic Law for Paul and Augustine. Fulgentius interprets this as a second step in personal and community development, receiving Augustine's take on the Pauline theme of the old self and the new self. Fullness of grace was obscured during the pre-Christian era, the time of the old self.[22] As a result of the full revelation of God's plan, the new person can live fully in the light of Christ, and in the fullness of the forms of grace now available. Fulgentius see Augustine;s stages of life under grace as another *uia*, leading one through the Christian life in a manner similar to the way of the Penitential Psalms.[23]

In collect 118.6, Fulgentius credits protective grace with enabling the individual to accept the law of God in its final revelation. The title, *defender of our souls*, expresses the dichotomy between the old Law, which, according to Paul and Augustine, was concerned with earthly things, and the new Law of the Spirit. One may live the life of the Spirit only through the initiative of grace as it converts one from sin.[24] The monastic community lives under this Law.

Salvific Grace

Collect 48 - *A man, the mediator of God and men has freed us. Therefore, redeem us though his grace from the hand of hell so that our meditation may be in you.*[25]

Collect 80 (complete) - *Calling to you in our distress, deliver us, we beg, by your gratuitous grace. You tested us at the waters of contradiction. Hear us in the darkness of the storm. Do not surrender us into the hand of our enemy, the devil, for you are the Lord our God, who led us out of the land of Egypt.*
Collect 113 - *[You] freed us from the idols of the nations, the works of the hands of men, transferred us into the kingdom of the light of your Son . . . grant us to live in you; grant us always to please you.*
Collect 114 - *We have been freed from the dangers of sorrow, death and hell through divine grace . . . deliver our eyes from tears . . . make us please you in the land of the living.*

Related to the actions of protective grace, salvific grace calls forth from Fulgentius phrases of soteriological import for his monks, a frequent theme in the collects.

Collect 48, by invoking the liberating and redemptive power of the Incarnation, draws the mind to meditation on the humanity as well as the divinity of Christ, God's presence within salvation. Thus, the fourth of Augustine stages of spiritual development (*in pace*), becomes the object of the collect's petitions. Continual mediation by the Son is necessary in order that the community may rest in that grace.

Fulgentius shifts the words of God to the psalmist from Ps. 80:8 into a petition that leads into an interpretation of several Exodus themes, including the "waters of contradiction" (Meribah)[26] and the "darkness of the waters," a reminder of the darkness of Egypt. In contrast to Israel, however, the community declares that they did not tempt God at the waters, but instead were tested themselves. The fact that two petitions follow indicate that the community passed its test, but that they still have a spiritual fear of the devil's further temptation. The conclusion of the collect is similar to the "reminder" portion of the lament genre, and reminds the monks of their constant need for gratuitous grace in their constant struggle against sin.[27]

Collects 113 and 114 offer an example of one of Fulgentius's "thematic pockets;" in this case, the two share the same expressions of grace theology. In addition to being freed from idols, the former collect evokes the darkness of Egypt by using phrase taken from Acts and Colossians.[28] The invocation against idolatry historically belongs to the period of the Exodus rather than to the fifth century; however, it forms an interpretative bridge in the spiritual interpretation of Egypt (the darkness of sin). Through the petitions, Fulgentius connects salvation history with God's grace. The same action that put people under the law of worship to the one God also preserves Christians from sin.[29]

In collect 114, Fulgentius pursues the same theme, indicating possible frustration on his part with the conciseness required by the collect form. Collect 114 provides treatise-like commentary on its predecessor. As a result of the grace petitioned in collect 113, the monks learn from what they are saved: death and hell. The petition for deliverance from tears recalls the "waters of contradiction" from collect 80, and both plead for life. Even though Ps. 114 is a hymn of praise with some wisdom elements and contains no Exodus references, the unity of divine inspiration in the psalter allows Fulgentius to carry compose an internal commentary among the collects. Salvific grace continues to free people from sin, as it freed them from Egypt.

Grace and Forgiveness

> Collect 6 - . . . *so that the holy angel may watch over our beds and reward our groans and tears with divine grace.*
> Collect 18 (complete) - *God, by the grace of your word, cleanse from our secret (faults?), and confirm what you deigned to effect in us, so that, cleansed from the great sin, the speech of our mouths might be pleasing in your sight.*

The orations repeatedly indicate that the monks had a strong sense of their own sinfulness.[30] Augustine's claim that corporeality is the primary human flaw inspires the spiritualization of the psalms by the collects. The strength and stability of the spirit allows it to transcend the limitations of the flesh and seek forgiveness for sin,[31] which finds its goal in grace.[32]

By accepting God's offer of forgiveness and salvation in Christ, the monks have rejected evil as unleashed in the world through Adam, and recognize their position as saved participants in the Body of Christ.[33] By invoking grace the monks can verbalize both forgiveness of sins and the motivation to avoid evil and do good. In conflict between spirit and flesh, the spirit is able to act through the gift of God.[34] The large number of references to sin indicates the monks' acute awareness of the ongoing struggle, and the need to be reminded of it at frequent intervals.

Forgiving grace, which also provides motivation for avoidance of sin, receives implicit treatment in collect 6. Its *quo* clause exhibits two unique features among the collects: it is the only collect to refer to an angelic being, and the only one to use the verb *remuneror*, "to pay back," or "reward." As this is also the first of the Penitential Psalms, Fulgentius may have deliberately opened the collection with an unusual term as a counterpart to the closing collect 142.

On the surface, Fulgentius's use of *remuneror* appears to conflict with Augustinian thought on the topic of gratuitous grace. Yet, Fulgentius's understanding of physical suffering (expressed, in this case through groans and tears), due to spiritual pain as a result of one's recognition of sinfulness, offer an explanation of what at first glance could indicate a lapse into the Pelagian camp. Instead of sleeping, the individual is suffering on his bed. Groans and tears indicate his honest appraisal of his sinful nature, and an unfettered release of sorrow. The level of suffering indicated in the collect is further enhanced by the use of the terms "groans" and "tears" together only in this collect.[35]

This non-verbal, yet eloquent expression of groaning brings out another Pauline interpretation. Rom. 8:18-27 refers to groans three times as testimony to the working of the Spirit deep in the individual's soul. Paul's text helps to explain the apparently unorthodox use of *remuneror*. In the face of such ingenuous expression, forgoing the needs of the body (sleep) in favor of the soul's raw emotional outpouring, the soul receives grace for giving itself over to Augustine's third stage (*sub gratia*). More divine grace appears in the fourth stage (*in pace*), in which the soul dwells in peace with no opposition from the body. Further influence from Rom. 8 provides Fulgentius with an argument for the orthodoxy of collect 6's grace theology. Paul begins the segment on the workings of the Holy Spirit with the Motivation: "I consider that the sufferings of the present time are not worth comparing with the glory that is to be revealed to us."[36] The first of the Penitential Psalm collects presents the temporal challenge in light of future comfort received from grace. Awaiting at the end of the penitential voyage through the depths of human sinfulness is the quenching of the body's desires, and the soul's ascent to full participation in divine grace.

The style of collect 18 is more representative of Fulgentius's usual theological style, being more obviously in the mainstream of Augustinian orthodoxy. The operations of grace as forgiveness and motivation appear more clearly here than in collect 6. Fulgentius evokes the third stage of spiritual development, for the collect requests the strength to continue the submission to grace. By cleansing the "great sin" (*delicto magno*), one's speech (*eloquia*) becomes pleasing. By connecting pleasing speech with cleansing of great sin, Fulgentius shows his concern with public and private talk among the monks, made all the stronger by the fact that the only other time *eloquia* appears in the collects is to refer to the Word of God.[37] Dissatisfied grumbling from monks, a practice to which Benedict would later prove no stranger,[38] indicates to Fulgentius the sin of pride, which perverts the gift of speech, over which much care must be taken.

Frequent Grace

> Collect 74 - *Visit us with frequent grace, God Almighty Father, so that, singing a psalm for you, we may destroy all the power of sin.*

The *Opus Dei* is here connected with obtaining grace; the community's prayer springs from grace that empowers them to request further grace to act against sin. Awareness of grace abounds in this community, and the collect affirms that prayer is the purpose of their common life. The collect's text seems to indicate that each psalm they sing gives its own grace, thus the number of psalms would be connected to a sense of frequently granted grace.

Eschatological Dimensions of Grace

> Collect 4 (complete) - *We call on you, God Almighty Father, for to you belongs all the grace we ask. Mark over us the light of your countenance, so that, having been found to be grain in the time of threshing, we might rejoice in the eternal storehouse of your sanctuary, filled with the oil of charity and the wine of apostolic doctrine.*
> Collect 98 - *Perfect in us, we beg, Lord, the work of your mercy, so that your people may not grow angry in your reign, but may merit to co-reign with you through your grace.*

Fulgentius invokes the human approach to God, rather than God's approach to humanity through the Incarnation,[39] allowing the monks to become active participants in the operations of grace. The divine countenance is the repository of grace in the form of light, a frequent Augustinian metaphor.[40] Fulgentius then employs an agricultural theme that makes connections to a Gospel parable[41] that requests the ultimate result of grace: eternal life in heaven, the eternal storehouse.

No invocation to Christ appears in collect 4, rather references to the "oil of charity" and the "wine of apostolic doctrine." Other than this influence, the role of the Incarnation in sharing the human with the divine is absent.[42] By appealing directly to the Father, Fulgentius offers a total spiritualization, approaching the essence of divinity itself without evoking the human agency of Christ, and reveals the community's longing for their portion of the eternal promise. The radical disposal of a direct reference to the divine sharing the human, they stress their uncompromising desire to directly partake in eternal life.

Collect 98 combines an invocation of the kingdom with a petition for grace. Here, the address of, "Lord" appears to bring in the identity of Christ. The petition to "co-reign" calls to mind the request of Zebedee's sons to reign on Christ's right and his left.[43] In this case, though, through their "white martyrdom" of monastic life further exacerbated by Vandal persecution, the monks could conceivably claim a right to feel that they have "drunk from the cup" from which Jesus drank. Politically disenfranchised by the Vandal kingdom on earth, loyal Catholics can request to co-reign with Christ in the kingdom of heaven.

Anti-Pelagian Formulas

Collect 10 - *In your power, make us quickly extinguish all the arrows of evil, made safe by the justice of your grace by which we have been saved by no preceding merits of our own.*
Collect 52 (complete) - *We are useless because of our sin; there is no one who does good, there is not even a single one. Therefore, Lord, raise up your grace in us, so that our bones may not please themselves.*
Collect 118.5 (complete) - *Grant, Lord, that, through your grace, we may abide in the truth that we chose and to adhere to your testimonies. May we not sleep in our sins, but keep watch in your precepts.*

The controversy that Augustine's *Epistola* 194[44] caused at the monastery at Hadrumetum, and the care Augustine took over his response to the community,[45] indicate the seriousness of theological issues among the monks. In these three collects, Fulgentius made his position on divine initiative in the area of grace clear, with no hint of divergent opinions.

Collect 10 indicates that Fulgentius will employ little subtlety in his rejection of heretical views. Free will is not forgotten, however. Grace allows the monks to "extinguish the arrows of evil," indicating their choice to accept God's grace and use it in their lives.

Free will also appears in collect 52. Sinfulness makes good works impossible; only through grace can the human will assert itself for good. By using the verb *suscite* ("to raise up"), Fulgentius teaches that grace arises within the individual and causes their free will to act properly: the individual pleases God rather than himself.

The connection between grace and free will appears in collect 118.5, for adhering to God's testimonies and keeping watch in God's precepts are results of petitions for grace. That the community lives *sub gratia* is revealed through their petition to God to "abide in the truth." They pray for awareness of both the law and of the operations of grace in their lives. The desire to live under grace arises from grace and needs the continual influx of grace in order to continue.

The Collects and Chalcedonian Theology

After Augustine, the next great influence on Fulgentius was the Council of Chalcedon (451). He alludes to the council's "Definition" through use of the terms *substantia, consubstantialis, natura* and *uerbum*[46] that coincides with the christological language of the council. These terms call forth a richness of expression and examination from Fulgentius, who manages to bypass the space limitations of the collect form to offer a virtual treatise on orthodox christology throughout the course of the series.

Substantia

> Collect 2 - . . . *for the entire passion of human substance fell by lot to Christ Your Son, while he was providing himself with it in the Virgin. Therefore, grant us, we beg, to live on in him of whom we are all members in part.*
> Collect 21 - . . . *in that little worm is our substance renewed in you by beauty and comeliness.*

Both collects use the term "substance" in connection with Christ's humanity, but without ignoring his divinity. Collect 2 affirms the "Definition's," "born of Mary the Virgin, *Theotokos* as to his manhood." Fulgentius has apparently studied the concept of *Theotokos* and connects it with the Church's kerygmatic understanding in his phrase: "the whole passion of human substance."[47] Also evoked is Cyril of Alexandria's *Second Letter to Nestorius.*[48] Fulgentius, trained in Greek, could have had access to the letter, or portions of it, as his collect echoes the letter's phrasing. His concentration of the intricacies of Greek theological discourse into a few words of a liturgical unit remains as a tribute to his literary and theological skills. The phrase, "of whom we are all members in part," affirms humanity's *homoousios* with Christ as well as the concept of the Body of Christ.

References to Christ's human substance in collect 21 are similar to those in collect 84 (using the term "consubstantial;" see below) in that Christ's divinity is also asserted. The collect includes an extraordinary reference to of Christ as "that little worm," referring to the ugliness of the concupiscent side of human nature, made beautiful by Christ's chaste assumption of it. Christ is here portrayed as a complete human being, possessing body and soul, yet one who rises above the dangerous temptations of the flesh (the "worm"). As such, he offers a model and challenge to his monks, affirming their ascetic life, but nonetheless reminding them of their need for penitence.

Consubstantialis

Collect 17 - . . . *by the consubstantial light of your Word.*
Collect 55 - *the Word, Your consubstantial Son.*
Collect 84 - . . . *so that your Truth, which has been raised up in our land according to the flesh, may give sweetness to those who are consubstantial with it.*
Collect 106 - . . . *so that, healed by your consubstantial Word . . .*
Collect 116 - . . . *the Truth, which is consubstantial and coeternal with You . . .*
Collect 118.13 - *the grace of Your consubstantial and coeternal Word.*

Fulgentius takes care to treat as many of the intricacies of the term of "consubstantial" as he can. Collects 17, 55, 106, and 118.13 attest to Christ's *homoousios* with the Father, and explore various aspects of Christian belief concerning the divine substance. Collect 17 evokes Jn. 1:4-9 and the Nicene-Constantinopolitan Creed with its reference to light, and collect 55 offers a paraphrase of the "Definition's" teaching: "*homoousios* with the Father as to his Godhead," Collects 116 and 118.13 not only confirm the community's acceptance of Chalcedon; they also form a portion of Fulgentius's active teaching against Arianism in the council's teaching: "begotten of the Father before ages as to his Godhead."[49]

Collect 84 appropriates the "Definition's," "the same *homoousios* with us as to his manhood," but does not let go of the union of human and divine, as the reference to "Your Truth" suggests.

Natura

Collect 59 - . . . *when he himself put on human nature.*
Collect 67 - *He, who having been clothed with human nature, ascends over the western horizon, Jesus Christ, your Son, who lives and reigns with you.*
Collect 87 - *Come to the aid of human nature, restored in Your only-begotten Son.*
Collect 118.22 - *By the love of Your Christ, which exists in both natures, confirm, Lord Almighty Father, the hearts of your household.*

Tertullian employed the single term *natura* as a translation for the Greek *hypostasis* and *physis*.[50] By the time of the correspondence between Leo I and Flavian of Constantinople, use of the term *natura* for *physis* had been regularized.[51]

As with *substantia*, Fulgentius uses *natura* primarily to evoke Christ's human nature. Collects 59 and 67 employ Paul's image of putting on "the new man,"[52] using both active and passive voices (compare collect 59 with collect 2's remarkable imagery). The community imitates Christ's assumption of human nature by renewing their human persons in Christ. Fulgentius, who cannot long meditate in Christ's human nature without reference to his divinity, brings a resurrection theme into collect 67 from the psalm's call to praise God, "who rises above the horizon."[53]

Collect 87 addresses salvation in a petition to God the Father. As in collect 21, which uses the term *substantia* to treat renewal theology, here, human nature receives renewal and restoration through Christ.

Christ as the Beloved Son appears in collect 118.22, in which Fulgentius again addressed both natures. The petition that follows makes its plea in light of Christ's love, which exists in the two natures. The reference to "Your household" affirms the ideal for which the monks strive in community and the heavenly realization of that household, the kingdom of God.

Verbum

Collect 59 - . . . *so that our strength might be in the strength of Your Word, who extended his shoe into Idumea.*

The connection of *uerbum* with *logos* appears in five collects: 17, 55, 106 and 118.13, which employ it in conjunction with *consubstantialis*, and 59, which uses it in an unmistakably christological manner.[54] "Idumea" (Edom) refers to Esau,[55] and serves as a contrast to the appearances of Jacob in the collects. The community identifies with Jacob, especially in his identity as "Israel," in signifying the dichotomy between spirit and flesh. The "strength" of collect 59 is that of the hypostatic union, overpowering the spiritual death, the result of life in the flesh, with the fullness of life in the Spirit.

CONCLUSION

In the hands of Abbot Fulgentius, later Bishop of Ruspe, the Psalm collect, a genre without too much obvious literary potential, becomes in the course of the *Africana* orations, a mirror of contemporary Catholic monastic life. Even though elegance of phrasing and literary development are at a premium, the forcefulness of expression and the commitment to orthodoxy and liberation, both temporal and spiritual, form the collection as a whole into a text of considerable rhetorical vitality. By effective use of *sermo humilis*, complex theological questions are reduced to simple phrases, teaching the essence of Christian belief.

Even though he lived a century after rigid liturgical canons had been promulgated in North Africa, Fulgentius shifted the existing reception mode for the Psalms into a focused temporal situation. His orations kept to most councillor requirements, the permission of the local bishop being the only one in question. Doctrinally, he kept to the Catholic teachings with admirable faithfulness.

Historical Placement

Despite his expected interest in the spiritual salvation of his monks, Fulgentius addressed the daily persecution that they all experienced. His skillfully veiled political references allowed the community to bring those concerns to prayer without attracting the attention of the Vandals or their sympathizers.

Other local concerns received ample attention as well. The farming practices of the region offered ample opportunities for metaphor to guide the community's meditations. Concern for the spiritually and temporally poor indicate the importance of showing charity to others.

Literary Technique

Consciuosly or not, Fulgentius's reception of the psalms in the collects employed literary techniques, especially in the areas of mimesis, classical reception, and catharsis. By adapting the classical techniques to Christian values, Fulgentius could receive a psalm verse with an intensely personal object in mind, be it spiritual, political theological, or temporal. The collects thus became a platform for guided meditation on the psalms, with specifically chosen verses supplying the scriptural basis for the mimesis that brings out the full revelation of Christ promised by the revelation of the psalm. Classical reception allows Fulgentius to exploit the more dramatic utterances of the psalter by addressing emotional aspects of their life together and by allusion to the Christian Scriptures, especially the Gospels and Pauline writings. The result was a catharsis of feeling among the monks, assuring them that constancy to their life would result in their receiving a place in the heavenly fatherland.

Fulgentius did not receive psalm genres in the same manner as modern form critics, tending even in the Hymns of Praise towards a uniform mood that form critics would associate with the lament psalms. The sub-genres of royal and wisdom psalms seemto engage his imagination in their discourse on Christ's Messiahship and Christian versions of the virtue of wisdom. Any Exodus reference interested Fulgentius, so much so that he created a genre of interpretation based on those references. He also received the penitential character of seven specific psalms that were later identified by Cassiodorus as forming a collection of Penitential Psalms.

Theology

The collects indicate an early and enthusiastic reception of Augustinian theology. There are no hesitations or questions on the topic of grace, like those at the Hadrumetum monastery or of the semi-Pelagian monasteries in Gaul. Grace in all its forms is a gratuitous gift, which no one may expect to earn.

Fulgentius also affirms the teachings of the Council of Chalcedon concerning proper christology, and instructs his monks in other orthodox forms of belief.

Fulgentius's later works indicate that his theological convictions remained strong throughout his life. The stylistic development and the sobriety of expression required of the bishop later in life have obscured his early work in the collects.

The Collects Today

The compilers of the modern Office book used by many apostolic Religious in the United States, *Christian Prayer*, have translated collects from the *Romana* and *Hispana* series for use in the book. However, they have merely paraphrased a few sentences of the *Africana* collects.[1] One cause for this omission may be the intensity of their imagery and expression of theological conviction, which are very much of their own time. The theological struggles of Catholics in Vandal North Africa do not directly address the spiritual and doctrinal concerns of our own century.

Yet, the *Africana* collects remain more than historical curiosities. They offer an indication of the breadth of literary activity in Late Antiquity, and offer the modern reader a glimpse of an original mind at work interpreting the prayer of the Church. Fulgentius of Ruspe did not break new ground in theological thought. His contribution to the Church was literary, polemical, and, above all, pastoral.

APPENDIX

The Collects in English

1.Visit us in your salvation, Lord, so that we may *meditate* continually *on your law day and night.* Build us . . . by your help of divine grace in every place of power, so that we may return to you *the fruits* of divine culture *in their time.*

2. May you never permit the most evil demon to go through our *lands,* for the entire passion of human substance fell by lot to *Christ your Son,* while he was providing himself with it in the Virgin. Therefore grant us, we beg, to live on in him of whom we are all members in part, so that *serving you,* God and Father, *in fear,* we may deserve to obtain the rewards of *blessedness.*

3. *Grind away,* Lord, *the teeth of sinners* and of our evil diabolic enemy, and *hear our voices from your holy mountain.* Therefore, *rise up* in our help, so that when all sins have been expiated and we have been warned by chaste messengers from on high, we *may not fear thousands* of evils.

4. We call on you, God almighty Father, for to you belongs all of the grace that we ask. Mark over us the light of your countenance, so that, having been found to be grain in the time of threshing, we might rejoice in the eternal storehouse of your sanctuary, filled with the oil of charity and adorned with the wine of apostolic doctrine.

5. All powerful eternal God, receive our words with your ears. You who hear the voice of our prayer before we ask you for what we seek, because it is your power both to will and to effect us by good will that we, armed with the shield of your good will, we might always do what is pleasing to you.

6. Lord, look upon the weakness of our nation, and heal our souls, because we have sinned against you, so that the holy angel may watch over our beds, may reward our groans and tears with divine grace.

7. Lord, rescue us from all persecutors, lest the most evil demon like a lion may take that which has been conferred on us by Christ. Iniquity descends upon his own head, so your people, purified from all sins, may sing to your name.

8. Perfect, Lord, the praise from the mouths of your children, and destroy the enemy of humankind. Save us, the works of your fingers, we beg, so that your name may be marvelous among the human race over all the earth.

9. In the gates of the daughter of Zion, God and Father, we bend the knees of our heart to you. Raise us, we beg, from the gates of death so that we may always exult in your praises.

10. Save us, Lord, confident in you, and grant to us through gratuitous gift to be better than many sparrows. In your power make us quickly extinguish all the arrows of evil, made safe by the justice of your grace by which we have been saved by no preceding merit of our own.

11. Keep us, Lord, from this generation unto eternity. Arise, we beg, on account of the misery of the needy and the groans of the poor and save your people.

12. Almighty eternal God, light up the eyes of our heart, and make us watchful of your precepts, so that our heart, exultant in your salvation, may say to you with total confidence: I shall sing to the Lord who has granted good to me.

13. God Almighty Father, remove the captivity of your people, and, we entreat, show to all the way of peace in him who made both things one, in which Jacob, our man, may exult in the flesh until, made Israel, he might merit to see you, God.

14. Lord, visit us who wander from you so long as we are in the flesh, and make us through gratuitous gift to be inhabitants of the eternal tabernacle. Let us never take money from the innocent. Grant to our littleness to give your money to the moneylenders, and not to demand this back with interest, but with crowns which are gratuitous gifts.

15. Always secure in your goodness, God Almighty Father, we cry out saying: The Lord is the portion of my inheritance and of my cup. Therefore keep us in your gratuitous grace and fill us with the joy of your countenance, so that our delight may always be in you.

16. Lord, protect your people under the shadow of your wings from the face of the hostile ones who plan an insurrection against our soul as the lion prepared for prey. Rise up, we beg, rise up, come before and scatter, so that we may appear in your justice before your face until your glory will be revealed.

17. Remove from us, Lord, the darkness of our sins. And illumine our hearts by the consubstantial light of your Word who abides in both his natures. Gird us, we beg, with virtue and show us the stainless way in Him.

18. God, by the grace of the Word cleanse from our secret, and confirm what you delighted to effect in us, so that, cleansed from the great sin, the speech of our mouths might be pleasing in your sight.

19. As we, unworthy as we are, assist at the heavenly offices, hear us, we beg, Lord, in the day of tribulation. And protect us from all evil, so that the spiritual Pharaoh may come to ruin in horses and chariots as we rise up. But may we exult in you, Lord our God.

20.Lord, we are singing your virtue with bodily tongue and bodily voice, make us, we beg, spiritual men from corporal, so that, perceiving spiritually from the carnal letter which kills, may we exult strongly, lest you deceive us of the will of our lips.

21. For our salvation Lord, make the words of our sins far from our salvation and renew us. In that little worm is our substance, renewed in you by beauty and comeliness, so that we might glorify your mercy and our praise might be in your presence in the great Church.

22. We are a new people instructed in doctrine, and place above the waters in the spiritual place of the eternal pasture, may your staff console us, we beg, which flowered in the house of Aaron and sprouted forth in the house of David according to the flesh from Mary Ever Virgin. Anoint our heads with the oil of this charity so that we

may live in your house through an infinite length of days.

23. Raise up, Lord, that the gates of your temple which is in us may be eternal. Let Christ the King of Glory enter them as if into heaven itself. And now he settles the wars of evil by spiritual, so that all of our earth and the souls that dwell in it may be yours.

24. Preserve our souls and free us, Lord, so that we who call upon you may not be confounded. May you not remember the sins of youth and ignorance, but be mindful of us according to your mercy.

25. God Almighty Father, do not destroy our life with men of blood, that we may be worthy and pleasing in your truth. Cause us not to go in with those who do iniquity, and to have hatred for the congregations of evildoers, so that our interior foot might walk in the right way and our tongue bless you in the assemblies.

26. Bestow abundantly on us, Lord, our illumination, so that we may dwell in your house all the days of our life. Save us, we beg, so that we may always offer to you the pleasing victims of jubilation.

27. Raising weak hands at your holy temple, we beg you, Lord, do not hand over our souls to sinners among those who do not acknowledge you. Do not destroy us with the workers of iniquity, do no desert us.

28. Strip us of our evils, Lord, and grant to us contrite and humble hearts to offer in place of the offspring of rams. May the voice of mercy sound over the vast waters which signify the peoples and nations so that in returning the stumblings which cause iniquity, you may bless your people with peace.

29. Save us, calling to you, Lord, so that we who weep in the evening to the Lord as if he were sleeping, when the same arises in us in the morning we may rejoice, so that bursting forth and clothed with rejoicing, our glory may always sing to you, Lord.

30. Incline, Lord, a pleasing ear to your servants, and be for us the God of protection. Remove us from the traps of those who lie in wait for us, so that your Church which is our life may always say to you:

You have redeemed me, Lord God of Truth.

31. From the pressures which had surrounded us, redeem us, Lord. We have acknowledged our sin and our injustices; you, pardon us!

32. Although we are not just, it is nevertheless just for us to rejoice in you, Lord Father Almighty God. Give us, therefore, to love you with an upright heart, so that the human substance of the whole earth may fear you, so that when the bitter waters of this world have been gathered as in a flask, the waters of your word may flow to us, for all of your words are established in faith.

33. Restrain our tongue from evil, Lord, so that your praise may always be in our mouth. Grant, we beg, to your people to seek and to follow your peace, so that you might watch over us with your eyes and your ears may attend to our prayers.

34. Seize arms and shield, and rise up for our help God Almighty Father. Redeem our souls from the tricks of the evil one, so that all our bones may say: Lord, who is like You?

35. It is your role, Father and Lord, to save people and beasts, that is, to save souls and bodies. May you not desert our cause, we beg, for the Samaritan doctor of the world carried all of us on his own beast. Have mercy on all; spare all; may we all merit to see the light in your light.

36. The man of human substance will never be able to seek better gifts, unless his steps shall have first been prepared by you, Lord. Therefore, Lord, prepare in us the things that are to be helped, and help the things that have been prepared, so that, escaping from your enemies like smoke, our hearts may always meditate on your wisdom.

37. Lord, omnipotent eternal God, do not convict us in your indignation because our soul is filled with illusions. Remove, we beg, your arrows from us and heal our bones.

38. Lord, light of our souls, watch our ways, so that there may be no punishable sins on our tongue, so long as that sinner, the enemy of our nature, stands against us. Allow us to amass not temporal, but eternal treasure. May they not be gathered elsewhere, but stored in

heaven.

39. Stretch toward us, Lord, who trust in you, and place our feet upon the rock, so that it might not be crushed by a storm of the world that comes upon it. Behold, we do not restrain our lips. May it be pleasing to you; free us, God Almighty Father.

40. Strengthen us in your sight, Lord, and do not betray us into the hands of the enemy, for you have already raised us up in Christ the Lord. Bring us help upon the bed of sorrow, and heal our souls, for we have sinned against you. Keep us and make us alive and make us blessed on earth.

41. May your virtue appear in us, Lord, so that our souls may no longer be sad. May your raging anger grow quiet through the suspension of your waves, so that, when the tranquility of your indulgence follows from you, we may daily desire God like the deer at the flowing waters.

42. Lord, send forth your light and your truth to our souls, so that we may always confess you in the lyres of our hearts. Decide our case against an unholy people, and save us in your strength.

43. All the day our shame is before us. Do not turn away our steps from your way, God Almighty Father. We have not spread out our hands to a strange God. Arise, we beg, arise to help us and redeem us because of your Name.

44. All the wealthy of the people have forgotten their nation and their father's house, God Almighty Father. We, your sons, have pursued comeliness and beauty; therefore, hear us and prosper us so that we may always be pleasing in your eyes.

45. Lord, we will not fear when our land is disturbed, for it has merited to hear in Christ your son: sit at my right hand. Revive us from dead works, so that, while mountains are carried into the depths of the sea, you, God, might be known in our houses.

46. Father Almighty God, we beg, save all the nations in whom the beauty of Jacob, whom you loved, has been assumed in Christ, so that, freed by your mercy and your might, we may rejoice in your

prayers and devoutly sing psalms to our God.

47. We know, Lord, that you are pious; hear what we speak in your towers and relieve our sighs, so that our hearts may be placed in your power; and may the whole Church always say to you: we received, God, Your mercy.

48. May the iniquity of our end not encircle us, Lord, for a brother will not redeem us, but a man, the mediator of God and men, has freed us. Therefore, redeem us through his grace from the hand of hell so that our meditation may be in you.

49. Free us, Lord, from every tribulation and grant to us that we may glorify you. Grant us always to return to you, Most High, our vows and to place the covenant above sacrifices.

50. Do not cast forth from your fate, God Father, what is yours, but rather, save us from our injustice. Give to us the joy of your salvation and confirm us with the guiding Spirit.

51. Accept the prayers of your household and make us fruitful olive trees in your house, so that we may be assured in your mercy, and may wait for your name in the sight of your holy ones.

52. We are useless because of our sin; there is no one who does good, there is not even a single one. Therefore, Lord, raise up your grace in us, so that our bones may not please themselves.

53. Lord, hear the words of our mouth with your ears, and see all the evils in the demon our most wicked enemy; convert the insurrections of the aliens, but save us, unworthy as we are, who trust in your name.

54. May we merit that the voice of the enemy and the tribulation might silence sinners, if you are already pleased, Lord, grant rest to your servants. Therefore, stretch to us, hear us, we beg, so we may heartily praise you in the evening and morning.

55. Lord, place our hearts in your sight, and save us from falling, so we may properly praise the consubstantial word, your Son, and please you in the land of the living.

56. Lord, look down upon those whom your right hand has planted, because our soul trusts in you. Protect us under the shadow of your wings until the iniquity of our vexatious sins has passed by.

57. Grant to all of us, we beg, to meditate on your justice, Lord, so that none will transgress from the womb, and no one will stray beyond the boundaries of your house. Restrain the teeth of the lions that destroy your flock; rise up and be present to defend the sheep for which the Good Shepherd laid down his life, through the same.

58. Visit us, Lord, in your gratuitous mercy, and rescue us from our enemies, so that we too, converted in the evening, may overcome them by the flesh itself, in which you only-begotten Son triumphed on the cross.

59. Lord, go forth in our strength, so that our strength might be in the strength of you Word, who extended his shoe into Idumea, when he himself put on human nature. Therefore, grant to us in him, aid from tribulation and bury the sins of your people.

60. Hear, Lord, the prayers of our entreaties, and have mercy on the troubles of your people, exalt us on that rock, the house of your grace, against which the gates of hell do not prevail.

61. We pour our hearts before you, God Almighty Father. The whole Church sings this to you, to you, God alone, subjecting its soul. Therefore, deliver us from our sins, so that the whole council of the people may always hope in you.

62. You know, Lord, what our thirsting soul, in the desert on account of our sins, desires. Fill us, God, with riches and fat, the gifts of your indulgence, so that the prayer of our heart may always be on you.

63. Protect us, all-powerful God, from the assembly of malicious people and the multitude of evildoers, so that we may worthily merit to announce your works and to praise you, the Creator of all things, with a right heart.

64. Hear us, our Savior, hope of all the ends of the earth and the

distant seas. Make us vessels of honor in your virtue, so that our flesh may come to you translated from death to life.

65. Attend, Lord, to our prayers, so that those who are bitter in themselves may not be exalted, so that we may bless you, our God, and the whole earth, filled with rain by our prayers, may adore you.

66. Lord, you have become the Way for all the saints. Help us, in your salvation, to know [the Way] in our land. May we be watered by the rain of his spirit; we bear fruit for you in a spiritual way.

67. Lord, look upon our earth, which awaits the voluntary rain of your indulgence, and strengthen what you deigned to work in us, so that he might make our journey to you successful, he who, having been clothed with human nature, ascends over the western horizon: Jesus Christ, your Son our Lord, who lives and reigns with you.

68. The sins of our imprudence are not hidden from you. Stretch forth, we beg, Lord, stretch forth to our souls and redeem them.

69. Lord, look upon the weeping of you supplicants and stretch forth in our aid, so that, once you have confounded all who seek our soul, your people may exult and rejoice in you.

70. From our youth and until old age and decline may you not forsake us, Lord, for it is the custom of your Church to ask for this, so that, vivified from many tribulations and evil that has been shown, we may always confess to you in the vessel of the psalms.

71. Do not despise the souls of your poor, Lord; let that one rescue us from the hand of the powerful one about whom the prophet sang; and may he rule from sea to sea in us, Jesus Christ our God, who with you lives and reigns.

72. Reduce, Lord, to nothing in your heavenly city, the image of those who reduced your image to nothing in their earthly city. But, grant us to cling to you, God, until we may deserve to enter the eternal sanctuary.

73. May your mercies tower over our sins, Lord, so you do not forget the souls of your poor forever. You, who are the Christ,

brought to nothing the head of the great dragon on the wood, through your power. Remember, we beg, your congregation, which you possessed from the beginning.

74. Visit with frequent grace, God Almighty Father, so that, singing a psalm to you, we may destroy all the power of sin. Humble in us what harms; exalt what flourishes.

75. May he who was made known in Judea not desert us, God Almighty Father, since from them he is clothed for us according to the flesh. Break the bow of strength, the shield, the sword and the war of spiritual evil through his power, and grant peace to all peoples.

76. To you, Lord, we cry with our voice; hear us in your mercy, and if all our enemies anticipated the vigils, may you not soon forget to have mercy on your household.

77. The miracles which you worked for our fathers are not hidden, God Omnipotent Father; you feed them with your manna and give them water to drink from the spiritual rock that carried the figure of Christ. Lead us out, too, Lord, in a column of cloud through the day and a column of fire through the night, until we cross over the sea of this world, and deserve to possess the land of the living through your grace.

78. May the groaning of prisoners enter into your sight, Lord, and may your mercies soon seize us. You have received in adoption the offspring of the dead. Do not surrender us to the sinner from our desire because of your name, lest the nations say: where us your God?

79. Be mindful, Lord, of those fed with the bread of tears, and sated with tears in measure, and come to free us from all necessities. Convert us to you, we beg; show us your face and we shall be saved.

80. Calling out to you in our distress, deliver us, we beg, Lord, through your gratuitous grace. you tested us at the waters of contradiction. Hear us in the darkness of the storm. Do not surrender us into the hand of our enemy, the devil, because you, Lord, are our God who led us out of the land of Egypt.

81. To your grace alone, Lord, is it given to deliver the weak and

poor man from the hand of the powerful ancient enemy. Therefore, we beg, free us your poor from his hand, because you will be the inheritance in all the nations.

82. Your enemies acted against the covenant, Lord. Do not allow the remnants of your people Israel to perish, for you promised to save them. Make your enemies, who wanted to possess your altar for themselves, like the dung of the earth. Fill their faces with ignominy, while your piety will look more swiftly to your inheritance.

83. You, Lord, grant blessing to your servants, to whom you deigned to give the law, so that, walking from virtue to virtue from you, our mind might ascend from the valley of weeping and bear the fruits of divine cultivation.

84. Lord, we beg you, melt the sins of your people, and remove the captivity of your people, Jacob, so that your truth, which has been raised up in our land according to the flesh, may give sweetness to those who are consubstantial with it, and bear fruit for you God and Father.

85. You, Lord, are gentle and mild. Incline your ear to our prayers; have mercy, we beg, have mercy on those who call to you all the day and save the children of your handmaid.

86. Revive us, Lord, from dead works, and perfect the foundation of the feet of our soul; place immediately on the holy mountains, so that in him who as our God on earth was made human, you may allow us to abide through infinite ages, so that he himself may abide in us who with you lives and reigns as God in unity with the Holy Spirit through all the ages.

87. Situated in labors from our youth on account of our sins, both friend and neighbor are made far from us; come, Lord, come to the aid of human nature restored in your only-begotten Son, according to which you deigned to sustain what has been recited.

88. Exalt, Lord, our horn in your good pleasure, so that we may continuously offer sacrifices of jubilation to the Lord our God. Grant us constantly to walk in the light of your countenance by the steps of the soul, and cause us to sing your mercies in eternity.

89. Accept, God Almighty Father, the humble works of our servitude, and look down upon us your servants and upon your work; grant to us the joy of your salvation for the days on which you humbled us. Take direction over us, so that the works of our hands may be right. Spread out for us the path which leads to heaven.

90. Our God, our refuge, save us, we beg, because we hope under your wings. Free us, we beg, from the trap of the hunters, and make the scourge far from the tabernacle of our souls.

91. Remove our reproach, Lord, and make us rejoice in the works of your hands, so that, whatever we are in your house, the planting of the divine apostle may flower always by faith, always by hope, always by charity, in the halls of your house.

92. Your testimonies, Lord, have been made very credible while we divide the mysteries of the Lord's dispensation that have been completed, for a long time announced by the prophetic mouth; and therefore, we beg, clothe us with beauty and strength, and grant us to please you forever.

93. Behold, Lord, you know the thoughts of people, that they are vain. Rise up against those who malign us, and do not ever desert the shepherds of your flock. Be raised up, you who judge the earth, so that your inheritance may never again be disturbed.

94. Look upon your people, Lord, and remove the hardness of our hearts, so that we may not tempt you, as those ancient peoples did who were deprived of eternal rest. Make us always to rejoice in you, Lord, so that you may save your people and the sheep of your flock.

95. Behold, Lord, your entire Church raised from earth to heaven, and made heaven itself. It sings unceasingly: all the Gods of the nations are demons, but the Lord made the heavens. Grant us, we beg, to offer such fruits of divine cultivation to you, to sing such songs of honor and glory to your holy name.

96. Protect, Lord, by your gratuitous grace, so that our land, rained upon with the dew of the Holy Spirit, may rejoice as you reign in us, so that, hating evil, we may love you, Lord our God.

97. In the lyre of our hearts and the voice of the psalm, we, your servants, perform our required service to you, asking from God the Father so that you may save us by our right hand and your arm, and in Christ, your salvation, now manifested to all the nations.

98. Perfect in us, we beg, Lord, the work of your mercy, so that your people may not grow angry in your reign, but may merit to co-reign with you through your grace, so that we may exalt you, Lord God, and adore the footstool of your feet.

99. These, Lord, are the sheep of your flocks, called by your grace. Grant to us, in every error of temptation, to you . . . and make us offer devoutly to you our confessions ceaselessly in hymns, for we acknowledge you as our creator.

100. Remove the evil object from our eyes, Lord, and cause us to walk in the midst of your house in our innocence. Take away pride which we admit is the beginning of transgression, so that the whole man may serve you in the immaculate way.

101. Our days will not vanish like smoke, God Almighty Father, because you have already looked favorably upon the adoration of the humble. Remove the groans of your prisoners and release the offspring of the dead from all their bonds.

102. Lord, you yourself knew our formation. Arouse in us the word of this prophecy according to the height of heaven from the earth. Confirm your mercy upon us, and make our sins as far from us as east is from west.

103. Place, Lord, a limit to the waters of the world, so that they may not return to cover the earth of your people; thunder forth, we beg, so that they may flee from your face, because the waters have entered our soul, and may all of us who have been saved by divine power sing to you, Lord, in our life.

104. Look down upon us, God Almighty Father, and lead us out of the darkness of this Egypt, so that there may be no weakling in out tabernacles. Spread the cloud for our protection until we may take the eternal fatherland. Lead your people out in exultation and your chosen ones in rejoicing.

105. Remove from us, Lord, the wrath of your anger, and cause us always to confess your name. Save your people from the perdition of Dathan and Abiram and those like them, for apart from you we do not adore another god. May we tell of your powers as we are able, and may we who are saved sing your praises.

106. Lead us, Lord, out of darkness and the shadow, for we have been often humbled in our injustices. Gather us together from the east and the west, from the north and the sea, to praise you, so that, healed by your consubstantial word, we may deserve to obtain the rewards of blessedness.

107. Accept, Lord, the prayers of your servants, and prepare for yourself our heart to praise your holy name. Grant us remedy from tribulations and grant us to offer you worthy thanksgivings in songs and psalms.

108. Made heirs of your blessings, Lord, may we not fear the curses of those opposed to you. Even if they spoke evil against our life, you, Lord, Lord, deal with me according to your great mercy.

109. In the midst of enemies, Lord, cause us to dominate, so that we, who have already merited to sit at your right hand in Christ, your son, our creator and Lord, may merit to possess the eternal fatherland with all the saints.

110. Grant us, Lord, to praise your works in the council and congregation of the just, done in truth and justice, so that you may preserve the redeemed in the Redeemer and may grant pardon to your people.

111. Make us powerful upon the earth, Lord, so that our soul may now live not for itself but for you. Grant to us, we beg, that we may desire in your commands the whole of the grace for which we ask.

112. Look down, Lord, we beg, and make us children to sin, but not by our minds, so that we may always say from the rising of the sun to the setting: may the name of the Lord be blessed.

113. Lord, renewer of human nature, who, through your gratuitous gift, freed us from the shadowy death of Egypt and from the idols of

the nations, the works of the hands of men, transferred us into the kingdom of the light of your Son, grant us to live in you; grant us always to please you.

114. We have been freed from the dangers of sorrow, death and hell by divine grace. We pray, God Almighty Father, that you would deliver our eyes from tears and our feet from stumbling, and make us please you in the land of the living.

115. Accept, Lord, the prayers of your household who believe in you; allow us always to offer the sacrifice of praise to you. Quickly destroy the bonds of the sons of your handmaid so that we may return our vows to you each day.

116. May all nations and people offer you praise, God and Father. Strengthen, we beg, your mercy over us, and may that Truth which is consubstantial and coeternal with you possess our hearts eternally.

117. The struggle invites us Christians to confess rightly, so that it may raise us up away from earthly things to heavenly things. And, therefore, we ask, God Almighty Father, the we, to, also may say by the Spirit by which the prophet: this is the day the Lord has made: let us exalt and be glad in it. And so, make us, Lord, to walk uprightly as in the daylight in regard to those who are outside. Grant us never to stumble on the stone which the builders rejected. Make us abide in the building of that house, where joining two people he is made the cornerstone; so that, as we abide in him we might remain our head, and we, for our part, might remain his members.

118.1 (aleph). Lead our ways to keeping your statutes, so that we may seek you with all our heart. And do not reject us from your precepts forever.

118.2 (aleph). Lead our ways to keeping your statutes, so that we may fully keep your commandments and always confess you in the rightness of the heart.

118.3 (beth). Lord, abundant giver of all good things, grant to us, that we may seek you in our hearts. And do not repel us from your commandments.

118.4 (gimel). Lord, by your gratuitous gift, place us, from inhabitants of the earth to citizens of the heavenly fatherland, and grant us to hasten unswervingly in your commands, so that when you give good things to your servants, our soul may live in you.

118.5 (daleth). Grant, Lord, that, though your grace we may abide in the truth which we chose, and to adhere to your testimonies. May we not sleep in our sins, but keep watch in your precepts.

118.6 (he). Purify us, Lord, from our sins, and lead us in your ways. Remove our reproach, we beg, and protect us in the way of your commandments.

118.7 (vav). Lord our strength, remove us from the wrath to come, and let your mercy come upon us. Grant us, in the sight of kings, to speak faithfully about your testimonies, and always to meditate on your commandments.

118.8 (zayin). We extend double palms to you, God Almighty Father, so that, mindful of us, your piety may console us in our humility. Even though our tedium kept us back from sinners who deserted your law, we may not turn away from your laws.

118.9 (chet). This, Lord, is our portion, that we may observe your law as you keep us. Stir us up, Lord, we beg, to confess to you the judgments of your justice, and make us to be partakers of all who fear you.

118.10 (teth). Lord of great mercy, teach us the learning and the knowledge which you poured out over the sons of men, so that we may place nothing before you and your love, but the law of your mouth over much gold and silver.

118.11 (yodh). Charity, creatrix of all things that exist, Lord, save us whom your hands fashioned and shaped, so that we may serve you, the Lord, with an immaculate heart and live in you who are life.

118.12 (kaph). May the light of your word, our Counselor, shine in us, Lord, so that, while you banish the delights of the enemy from our hearts, we may keep the testimonies of your mouth.

118.13 (lamedh). May the grace of your consubstantial and coeternal Word remain in us, Lord, through whom all things have been ordered and founded, so that all things may serve you from generation to generation.

118.14 (mem). Lord, Redeemer of our souls, hold back our feet from every evil way, so that your law might be our meditation all the day.

118.15 (nun). Accept, Lord, our words of our mouth, and teach us your judgments, so that, even if sinners have placed a trap for our feet, we may not wander from your precepts.

118.16 (samekh). Lord, defender of our souls, grant to us to love you law and to hate enemies, so you do not confuse us from our expectations, but protect us through your gratuitous grace.

118.17 (ayin). Because it is the time for acting, and because the evil ones have destroyed your law, grant to us, we beg, God Almighty Father, to love your precepts more than gold and chrysolite, and to hate every evil way.

118.18 (peh). Redeem us from falseness, and direct our way to you, God Almighty Father, so that all iniquity may not dominate us whom your majesty has already deigned to free by your gratuitous gift.

118.19 (sadhe). Save us in the strength of your arm, because our enemies have forgotten your words, so that the fire of your word may consume our sins, and the brilliance may illumine our hearts.

118.20 (qoph). You, Lord, always prepare what you are to help; we beg, may our eyes hasten to meditate upon your words, so that you might hear the voice of your people, and grant us to guard the decrees of your clemency.

118.21 (taw). Grant us always to offer hymns of divine cultivation to your, Lord, so our souls may live and praise you, and not forget your commandments.

118.22 (shin). By the love of your Christ, which exists in both natures, confirm, Lord Almighty Father, the hearts of your household, so that we may always exult in your words as one who has found much spoil. Even though princes have persecuted us without cause, may we not be anxious about your words.

119. Hear the call of our tribulations, Lord, and deliver our souls from unjust lips. May you not allow those who hate peace to wage war upon us without cause.

120. Guard our coming in and going out, Lord, and mercifully grant whatever grace you know your children need to arrive at salvation.

121. Lord, Creator of all that exists, establish our feet in your sanctuaries; build the heavenly Jerusalem in us, so that member may be united to member by divine grace, and there might be peace in your power and abundance in your towers.

122. Like useless servants, we have our eyes on you. We cry out, saying: have mercy, Lord, have mercy on us; guard us, your servants, and look upon us who have contempt heaped upon us.

123. Behold, like a sparrow our life has been rescued from the deadly snare. We beg you, Lord our God, not to hand us over to be hunted for our sins, for we have placed our help in your name.

124. Lord, may your eyes be open upon your house day and night, so that you might allow no one of those who trust in you to be moved. Make us good and just and ready for every good work.

125. May the seeds of justice germinate in your sight. We sow these seeds with tears in your sight so that we might reap in joy what we await in patience, since you are the farmer.

126. Look down, Lord, and guard, so that what cannot be guarded in us unless you guard, build what cannot be finished unless you build it, so that we, having become your inheritance in all things, might not be confounded while they will speak with our enemies at the gate.

127. Lord, remove your scourges from us and cause us to fear you and to walk in your ways, so that, flourishing in a circle around your table like young olive trees, we may see the good things that are in

Jerusalem all the days of our lives.

128. Up to this time, no one has gained power over your Church, often besieged from its youth by terror and the war of spiritual evil. May you allow no one to overpower, God Almighty Father, so that we may be defended by the divine fortifications, and the gates of hell may not prevail against us.

129. May our ears be attentive, Lord, we beg, to our supplications, and hear the voice of our entreaty. Forgive our iniquities, and redeem Israel, your people, from its tribulation.

130. Knowing that our own sin is before us, our heart is not exalted, Lord. Raise to the heights what is laid low before you, the Lord, because we have hoped in you from this time until the end.

131. Grant us, Lord, we beg, to find a place for you, the Lord, to prepare a place for you in our hearts, so that when your priests have put on salvation, and the poor are sated with bread, your sanctification may flourish over us . . . already obtained of the Church.

132. Fulfill our servitude to you, Lord, and grant us all to live as brethren in unity, in you who are our peace. Make us good, we beg. Make us joyful and ready for every good work.

133. In the sanctuaries of your house, make us, Lord, always life up clean hands to you and bring you the pleasing fruits of divine cultivation.

134. Lord, come to the help of the prayers of the humble, whom you elected in the inheritance of your vine. May we always praise our Lord. Remove hardness from the face of our land; raise in us the clouds of apostolic teaching, and make our least please you.

135. Lord, look upon the affliction of your people, long troubled, and reveal yourself to free us by a strong hand and arm, so that when the spiritual Pharaoh has been conquered and we have obtained the land of our people as an inheritance, we may all say in our humility: May our Lord be mindful of us.

136. Accept the pious weeping of your household, Lord, and dismiss the harps of our captivity. May you not permit us to sing your song much longer in a foreign land. Restore all of us. Spare all of us. May we all deserve to possess the heavenly Jerusalem with all the saints.

137. Look down, Lord, from your holy heaven, so that we may always confess to you in all our heart. Hear all the words of our mouth and forgive the sins of your people.

138. Our soul will know, Lord, your wonderful works. Our mouth is not concealed from you. Loosen all our newest and forgive the old; illumine in us what is dark; lead us in the eternal way.

139. We bend our knees to you, God Father. Do not hand us over to the sinner because of our desire. Remove us from the hands of the evil one, that is, the ancient enemy. Free all from him. Grant to all. Arm all against his wiles.

140. May our prayer ascend in your sight, Lord, like incense, and may your mercy descend over us. Guard us from the snares that work evil. Grant consolation to all. Guide all. May we all merit to find pardon in your presence.

141. We pour out our entreaties in your sight. Do not desert us, God Almighty Father. Free us from those who persecute us, because that have been strengthened against us. Save us by your gratuitous mercy, because you are our portion.

142. We hasten to make satisfaction to you for our sins, lest you enter into judgment with your servants, God Almighty Father. Rescue us from all evil because no man will be justified in your sight, so that we may be saved by divine grace and your good Spirit may lead us in the right way.

143. Deliver us from the hand of alien sons and cause us to sing you a new song about them. Free us from the many waters, and grant to us to conform to your precepts.

144. Lord, deign to hear the prayers of your people: praise my soul, the Lord.

145. May our prayer enter into your sight, God Almighty Father, and keep your truth in us. Loosen, we beg, those who are bound. Lift up the fallen; protect the catechumens; receive the widows and the orphans; destroy the way of our sins so that our soul may always praise you in your holy temple.

146. Heal the sorrows of the people, God Almighty Father, and gather all their dispersions. Bind up our sorrows by the gift of your mercy, so that we may always begin in confession to you.

147. Remove, Lord, fear and the wars of spiritual worthlessness, and once you have been pleased, establish our borders in peace. Strengthen the bolts of the gates of your house, and do not allow the sons of darkness to prevail against us any longer.

148. Missing from manuscript.

149. . . . you may place the boundary, may you spare whatever loves, so that we all, made children of Zion, may deserve to obtain the eternal inheritance in place of temporal desires.

150. With well-sounding cymbals out of love for God and neighbor, we greatly praise you, God Almighty Father, in your saints, in the firmament of your power, for you are found with difficulty where you are, but with greater difficulty where you are not. Be merciful to your people, we beg. Change the mourning of all into rejoicing. Direct our hearts. Cure the wounds of all. Forgive the sins of all. Grant also rain to your land in its own time. Avert your anger from us. Grant abundance to your people. Suppress war and heresies. Extinguish schism everywhere, so that we may be helped with divine consolation in all things and through all things, and our spirits might praise you always.

NOTES

Preface

1. E. Gibbon, ed. J. Bury, *The Decline and Fall of the Roman Empire* (New York: The Heritage Press, 1962), 1, 44-45.

Introduction

1. See Exod. 4:11-12 for an example of miraculous persuasion and inspired speech.

2. George Kennedy, *Classical Rhetoric and Its Christian and Secular Tradition* (Chapel Hill, NC: The University of North Carolina Press, 1980), 120-124.

3. Both Paul's address on the Areopagus (Acts 17:22-31) and his defense before King Agrippa (Acts 26:2-23) can be analyzed in terms of argument, *ethos* and *pathos*.

4. Matt. 5-7.

5. See preface, p. xii.

6. Kennedy, *The Art of Rhetoric in the Roman World* (Princeton: Princeton University Press, 1972), 351-61.

7. Justin Martyr's *First Apology* is more a philosophical treatise than a rhetorical justification, although his defense against charges in chapters one to twelve contains elements of rhetoric. Tertullian's *Apology* is more rhetorical in style, especially in chapters one to three. He address the senate and emperor of Rome in terms reminiscent of Cato or Gracchus, but with the aim of persuading them of the validity of the Christian life. This portion of his writings has led commentators to assume that Tertullian was a lawyer.

8. M.C. Clark, *Rhetoric at Rome* (London: Cohen and West, Ltd., 1953), 149-150.

9. See Paul on problems of allegiance in 1Cor 1:11-12.

10. For a recent (and admittedly interim) study on the use of the psalms at this period in the early Church, see G. Woolfenden, "The Use of the Psalter by Early Monastic Communities," *SP* 26, (1993): 88-94.

11. B. Childs, "Psalm Titles and Midrashic Exegesis," *JSS*, 16 (1971): 137-150; A. Guilding, "Some Obscured Rubrics and Lectionary Allusions in the Psalter," *JTS*, 35 (1934): 41-55; J. Sawyer, "An Analysis of the Content and Meaning of the Psalm Headings," *Transactions of the Glasgow University Oriental Society*, 22 (1967-68): 26-38; E. Slomovic, "Toward an Understanding of the Formation of Historical Titles in the Book of Psalms," *ZAW*, 91 (1979): 350-380.

12. Important studies on Jewish liturgy and its influence on Christian liturgy include: C. W. Dugmore, *The Influence of the Synagogue on the Divine Office* (Westminster: The Faith Press, Ltd., 1944); A. Finkel, "Yabneh's Liturgy and Early Christianity" (*JES* 18, 1981, 231-250); E. Werner, *The Sacred Bridge* (New York: Columbia University Press, 1959).

13. Pss. 40:14; 71:18-20; 88:53; 105:48; 150.

14. *Gloria patri et filio et spiritui sancto, sicut erat in principio et nunc et semper in saecula saeculorum.* Eastern Orthodox usage has omitted, "as it was in the beginning," as compromising to its Trinitarian theology. Werner, *The Sacred Bridge*, 299; T. Ware, *The Orthodox Church* (Middlesex: Penguin Books, 1963), 216-233.

In Western monastic usage, the doxology was recited after each psalm. A reference to this practice appears in Cassian's *Institutiones coenobiorum*, 2.11 (*CSEL* 17, 26-27).

15. P. Battifol traces the development of antiphon texts to the eighth century in *A History of the Roman Breviary*, trans. A. Baylay (New York: Longman, Green and Co., 1912), 71.

16. 2Chr. 20:19-20. Commentary on the practice appears in Werner, *The Sacred Bridge*, 146, 345, 370.

17. Eph. 5:19 refers to "addressing one another in psalms, hymns and spiritual songs." J. Jungmann, offers a brief history of Christian usage in *Pastoral Liturgy* (New York: Herder and Herder, 1962), 57.

18. Ps-Athanasius, *De uirginitate siue Ascesi* (*PG* 28, 275). Written circa 370, this is the earliest known testimony to the practice of reciting psalm collects.

19. Aetheria, *Itinerarium*, 24 (*CSEL* 39, 71-74).

20. Cassian, *Institutiones coenobiorum*, 2.7, 3.7 (*CSEL* 17, 22-26; 41).

21. *La Règle du Maître*, 33.44, trans. and ed. A. de Vogûe (Paris: Les Éditions du Cerf, 1964), 2, 184.

22. L. Brou, *Psalm Collects from V-VI Century Sources* (London: Harrison and Sons, Ltd., 1949), 10. A single collect (not a psalm collect) was recited at the end of the hour of prayer, corresponding to a memorial or to the previous Sunday. The liturgical reforms of Vatican II included the option of reciting psalm collects. The National Conference of Catholic Bishops, in *Christian Prayer: The Liturgy of the Hours*, (New York: Catholic Book Publishing Co., Inc., 1976) approved the introduction of psalm collects (now called "psalm prayers") into the Office used in the United States and some other English-speaking countries. While some of the psalm prayers are newly-composed, others are direct translations from either the *Romana* or *Hispana* series (both series are included with the *Africana* series in Brou's *Psalm Collects*). Several prayers have been paraphrased from the *Africana* series.

Psalm collects do not address the liturgical season or memorials, as do antiphons.

23. Brou, *Psalm Collects*, 73-227.

24. H. Jauss, *Aesthetic Experience and Literary Hermeneutics*, trans. M. Shaw (Minneapolis: The University of Minnesota Press, 1982), 34; R. Holub, *Reception Theory* (London: Methuen, 1984), 75. The term for mimesis in classical literary criticism is *poiesis*.

25. The forms of Benedictions 4, 5, 6, 7, 8, 9, 11, 12 and 16 especially correspond to that of collects.

26. E. Auerbach, *Literary Language and Its Public* (London: Routledge and Kegan Paul, 1965), 46; Jauss, *Aesthetic Experience*, 64-68. The term for reception in classical literary criticism is *aisthesis*.

27. In hermeneutical terms, the "bridge" that the *Africana* collects offer is one that takes themes from various verses in each psalm. The collect author places the selected verses into a Christian context, thus drawing the monks' attention to them. By further placing the verses into the community's own *sitz im leben*, he produces a cathartic effect, allowing the monks to feel their situation with more urgency, placing their needs in front of God in the period between psalms.

28. Augustine, *Confessiones* 1.13 (*CCSL* 27, 11-12).

29. Holub, *Reception Theory*, 78 and Jauss, *Aesthetic Experience*, 35. The term for the hermeneutical bridge in classical literary criticism is *catharsis*.

30. Augustine, in *De baptismo*, 6.26 (*CSEL* 51, 323) refers to the

writer of *formulae* that contain errors as *homines imperiti et loquaces*.

31. *CCSL* 149, 39.

32. *CCSL* 149, 28-29; C. Vogel, *Medieval Liturgy* (Washington, D. C.: The Pastoral Press, 1986), 34.

33. For a reflection on the use of creative thought in identifying genres, see A. Marino, "Towards a Definition of Literary Genres," in *Theories of Literary Genre*, ed. J. Strelka (University Park, PA: Pennsylvania State University Press, 1978), 42; H. Jauss, *Towards an Aesthetic of Reception*, trans. T. Bahti (Minneapolis: University of Minnesota Press, 1982), 10.

34. W. Frend's study, *The Donatist Church* (Oxford: The Clarendon Press, 1952), remains an admirable introduction to the conflict.

35. This study takes the position that the theological movements it addresses have political and social aspects to them as well as religious. Distinguished authors have taken the position that such movements were overwhelmingly theological, with few, if any, social catalysts. Among these authors: A. H. M. Jones, "Were Ancient Heresies National or Social Movements in Disguise?" *JTS* 10 (1959): 281-298.

36. For a brief survey of the use of *sermo humilis* by Greek and Latin preachers, see R. MacMullen, "A Note on *Sermo Humilis*," *JTS* 17 (1966): 108-112.

37. E. Auerbach, *Literary Language*, 32.

38. P. Brown, "Christianity and Local Culture in Late Roman North Africa," *JRS* 58 (1968): 91.

39. MacMullen, "A Note," 112.

Chapter 1

1. Brou, "Etudes sur les collectes du psautier: 1. La Série africaine et l'Evêque Verecundus de Junca," *Sacris Erudiri*, 6 (1954), 73-95.

2. *PL* 67.

3. *Vita Fulgentii* (*PL* 65, 117-150).

4. *PL* 67, 949-962. See P. Godet, "Ferrand Fulgence," *DTC* 5, 2, 2174-75, for further biographical information.

5. *Pro defensione trium capitulorum* (*PL* 67, 624).

6. *PL* 67, 889-908.

7. *PL* 67, 891.

8. *PL* 67, 910-921.

9. In *Ep.* 5 (*PL* 67, 910), Ferrandus mentions that Ps. 38:1 was sung in a monastery.

10. *PL* 67, 527-582.

11. *PL* 76, 867-878.

12. Brou, "Etudes," 95.

13. G. Bardy, "Verecundus," *DTC* 15, 2, 2672.

14. *CC* 93, 1-203. This is the only extant work of Verecundus that relies heavily on scriptural citations. His other works include the poems *Exhortatio Poenitendi* and *Crisias* (*SS* 132-165), and *Excerptiones de gestis Chalcedonensis concilii* (*SS* 166-185).

15. Brou includes a comparative chart in "Etudes," 77.

16. (*CC* 93, 28-29).

17. *CC* 93, 83-116; Collect 118.15.

18. *CC* 93. 4, 6 and 15.

19. Brou, "Études," 80-81.

20. *Bellum nequitiae spiritalis* (collects 23, 75, 128, and 147; *CC* 93, 6, 44, 68, 73, and 96); *nequissimus* (collects 2, 7, and 53; *CC* 93, and 69); *nubes apostolicae doctrinae* (collect 134, *CC* 93, 177). The last phrase also appears in an anonymous sermon written after Augustine's time: J. Leclerq, "Les inédits africains de l'homilaire de Fleury," *Revue bénédictine* 58 (1948): 57.

21. R. Demeulenaere, the editor of *CC* 93, subscribes to Brou's identification of Verecundus as the collect author (*CC* 93, xi-xiii and notes throughout the volume).

22. *Excerptiones de gestis* (*SS* 166-185).

23. Ferrandus, deacon of Carthage, *Vie de Saint Fulgence de Ruspe*, ed. P. Lapeyre (Paris: Lethielleux, 1929). A new English translation of the *Vita* and several theological works by Fulgentius is expected in late 1997 in the *Fathers of the Church* series.

24. Lapeyre, *Vie*, vii.

25. J. Palanque, *Le christianisme et l'occident barbare* (Stuttgart: Calver Verlag, 1966), 202-203. The name of Claudius's brother remains unknown.

26. Lapeyre, *Vie*, 10-13.

27. Ferrandus does not specify the ages at which Fulgentius joined the monastery, or when he was elected bishop of Ruspe.

28. H. Diesner, *Fulgentius von Ruspe* (Stuttgart: Calver Verlag, 1966), 17-19.

29. S. Stevens "The Circle of Bishop Fulgentius," *Traditio* 38 (1982): 327.

30. *De ueritate praedestionis* (*CC* 91A, 458-548), and *Ad Monimum*, 1.21 (*CC* 91, 20-21). In addition to using the term *gratia gratuitu*, Fulgentius uses *gratia munere*.

31. *Compluo*, "to drench with rain," found in collects 67 and 96, and in Fulgentius's *Sermo* 1 (*CC* 91A, 891). See A. Souter, *A Glossary of Later Latin* (Oxford: The Clarendon Press, 1949), 66.

32. The theory that an even younger Fulgentius was the mythographer of the same name is discussed in L. Whitbread, *Fulgentius the Mythographer* (Columbus, OH: Ohio State University Press, 1971), 3-5.

33. Fulgentius's polemical texts, *Ad Thrasamundum* and *Dicta regis Thrasamundi* are his earliest recorded works. See J. Fraipont's introduction and chronology in *CC* 91, v-xi.

34. Fulgentius's preeminence in theology is discussed by P. Godet in "Fulgence de Ruspe" (*DTC* 6, [1]), 968.

35. *People and beasts you will save, Lord.*

36. *It is your role, Father and Lord, to save people and beasts, certainly to save soul and body.* The parallelism of human and beast, body and soul, is carried through in the reference to Christ as the Samaritan.

37. *CC* 91, 65-94.

38. The debates between Thrasamund and Fulgentius must have been something of a spectacle. Such tension between the king's temporal power and the bishop's oratorical ability (only infrequently present in his extant writings) and theological knowledge certainly provided an intriguing mismatch. See C. Courtois, *Les Vandales et l'Afrique* (Paris: Arts et Metiers Graphiques, 1955), 302; Stevens, "The Circle," 327.

39. The catena consists of quotations from Prov. 8:22; John 16:29; Ps. 2:7; John 1:14; Col. 1:15.

40. Interestingly, Fulgentius does not employ what would seem to be the perfect text, the hymn from Phil. 2:5-11. He uses verses 10-11 of the hymn in *Ad Thrasamundum* 3.34 (*CC* 91, 181), but these verses do not address the crux of the christological argument. He uses verse 6 alone in the *Responsiones* (*CC* 91, 151). Was the Philippians hymn just too obvious, or was Fulgentius using more arcane scriptural references to show off?

41. *CC* 90, 6-7.

42. *CC* 90, 22-24.

43. *CC* 91A, 661.

44. *CC* 91A, 692.

45. *CC* 91A, 508.

46. The catena consists of quotations from Jn. 17:11, 15; Ps. 126:1; Phil. 4:7; Jer. 17:21; Ps. 24:20; Ps. 11:8; Ps. 120:5, 8, 4.

47. See Augustine's *Ep.* 130.1.1 (*CSEL* 44, 40-41), which, with its evocation of hope, connects to the ideals of collect 24, and *De sermone Domini in Monte*, 2.3.14 (*PL* 34, 1275). The collect itself draws from the mood of hope in the psalm. See also H. Chadwick, *Augustine* (Oxford: Oxford University Press, 1986), 72-74.

48. The use of biblical characters as surrogates for the Vandal rulers is discussed further in chapter 3.

49. The question of the identity of Fulgentius the Mythographer goes beyond the scope of the present study. Certainly, if he is the same person as the collect writer and the Bishop of Ruspe, the temperance called for would have resulted in further loss of possible literary gems.

Chapter 2

1. B. N. lat. 13159.

2. L. Brou, *Psalter Collects*, 21. Brou also edited two other series of collects, *Romana* and *Hispana*. He named the series after the first words of collect 1, which, in the *Africana* series are *Visita nos*.

3. *MS Hofbibliothek* 1861, *Goldener Psalter Karls des Grossen*.

4. *MS Douce*, 59. This manuscript differs in many ways from the psalter under present consideration. The pages of purple vellum and the golden ink allowed its scribe to produce a work of elegant beauty, quite different from the more rough-hewn style of that Paris psalter.

5. *Exaudi Christi. R. Carlo excellentissimo et a Deo caro [+ et a Deo caronato] atque magne et pacifico regi Francorum et Langobardum ac patricio Romanorum, uita et uictoria.* See V. Lerquais, *Les psautiers manuscrits latins de bibliothèques publiques de France* (Macon: Protat Frères, 1940), 2, 113.

6. The drawings in the psalter, skillfully rendered in pen and ink, show the plait motif, imaginary dog-like beasts, birds, serpents and a mermaid. See E. A. Lowe, *Codices antiquiores: A Paleographical Guide to latin Manuscripts Prior to the Ninth Century*, Vol. 5 (Oxford: Clarendon Press, 1970), 38.

7. Leroquais, *Les psautiers*, 2, 113.

8. Lowe, *Codices antiquiores*, 5, 38.

9. J. M. Canas Casas, *Las Colectas de Salmos de la Serie "Visita Nos"* (Salamanca: Universidad Pontifica, 1978), 39-40. The saints named are: Géréon of Cologne, Aldegonde of Maubeuge, Gertrude, Abbess of Nivelles [near Nimur], Lambert, bishop of Tongres-Maestricht [Liège], Bavo of Gand, and Afra of Augsburg. See Lowe,

Codices antiquiores, 5, 38.

10. Brou, *Collects,* 22.

11. The third hand in the manuscript does not use Carolingian minuscule.

12. Corrections appear in collects 5, 10, 14, 39, 43, 45, 52, 59, 61, 64, 65, 70, 78, 81, 84, 86, 92, 96, 98, 99, 103, 106, 109, 111 and 116.

13. Hereafter, Ver.

14. *Vindiciae canonicorum Scriptorum Vulgatae Latinae editionis,* ed. Giovanni Bianchini (Rome, 1740).

15. P. Capelle, *Le texte du psautier latin en Afrique* (Rome: Pustet, 1913), 83 and 133.

16. Among the terms peculiar to Africa are: *iucundarem, emendare, generare, collogere, altissimus,* and *grenium.*

17. Casas, *Las Colectas,* 124.

18. The Vandal kings ruled in succession from 428-534: Gaiseric (428-77), Huneric (477-84), Gunthamund (484-96), Thrasamund (496-523), Hilderic (523-30), and Gelimer (530-34).

Primary source material on the Vandals can be found in Victor of Vita, *Historia persecutionis* (*CSEL* 7) and Procopius of Caesaria, *De bello vandalico,* trans. H. B. Dewing (Cambridge, MA: Harvard University Press, 1953).

For secondary material on the Vandals and the migrations that culminated in their conquest of North Africa, the following works stand out: C. Courtois, *Les Vandales et l'Afrique*; P. Courcelle, *L'Histoire litteraire des grandes invasions germaniques* (Paris: Études augustiniennes, 1964); H. Leclerc *L'Afrique Chrétien* (Paris: Librairie Victor Lecoffre, 1904); F. Martroye, *L'occident à l'époque byzantine* (Paris: Librairie Hachette, 1904); L. Musset, *The germanic Invasions* (London: Paul Elek, 1975).

On the history of federating Germanic tribes, see G. Ladner, "On Roman Attitudes Toward Barbarians in Late Antiquity," *Viator* 7 (1976): 1-26.

19. Victor of Vita, *Historia persecutionis* 1, 3-4 (*CSEL* 7, 1-2).

20. Ulfilas's missionary journey to the Germanic tribes began during the reign of the Arian Emperor Valens (364-378). See Musset, *The Germanic Invasions,* 12, 184, and J. Jungmann, *Pastoral Liturgy,* 16.

21. Musset, *The Germanic Invasions,* 184.

22. Musset, *The Germanic Invasions,* 187-88; Leclerc, *L'Afrique Chrétienne,* 1, 153.

23. C. Julien, *Histoire de l'Afrique du Nord* (Paris: Payot, 1951), 1,

246.

24. The decline of Donatist influence after 411 did not cause the number of Catholic bishops to decrease.

25. J. Gavigan, *De uita monastica in Africa septentrionali* (Rome: Marietti, 1962), 57. See also Courtois, *Les Vandales*, 295.

26. *Historia persecutionis*, 3.41 (*CSEL* 7, 92). *Passio septem monachorum* (*CSEL* 7, 108-14).

27. *Historia persecutionis*, 3.3-14 (*CSEL* 7, 72-78).

28. H. Diesner, *The Great Migration* (London: Orbis, 1978), 127.

29. Ferrandus, *Vie de Saint Fulgence*, 84-85.

30. *Inimicus* appears in collects 8, 36, 38, 40, 54, 58, 76, 82, 109, 118.12, 118.19, and 126; *hostis* appears in collects 3, 53, 80, 81, 82, and 139; *iniquus* (as substantive referring to persons) appears in collects 25, 27, 28, 118.16, and 118.17; *malignus* (as substantive referring to persons) appears in collects 25, 63, 93 and 139; *persequentes* appears in collects 7 and 141; *princeps* (as persecutor) appears in collect 118.22; *alienus* appears in collect 53. See A. Souter, *Glossary of Later Latin*, 207, 240.

31. Collect 80.

32. Collect 53.

33. Collects 81 and 139.

34. Collect 8.

35. Collect 38.

36. Ps. 82:2 refers to *your enemies*. Collect 36, which also uses the term *inimicus* takes it from the third person reference of Ps. 36:20 and places it into the second person.

37. Collects 40, 54, 58, and 109.

38. C. Westermann, *Praise and Lament in the Psalms* (Atlanta: John Knox Press, 1981), 215.

39. Forms of *custodio*, used similarly to collect 126, appear also in collects 120 and 122, forming one of Fulgentius's thematic pockets. The term also appears in collects 11, 24, 38 and 140.

40. Ps. 118:113, 126.

41. Courtois, *Les Vandales*, 302-304.

42. Collects 2, 7 (in this collect, the demon works *with* the evildoers), 53 and 95.

43. Collect 100.

44. Collects 33 and 108. See W. Frend, "The Gnostic-Manichaean Tradition in Roman North Africa," *JEH* 4 (1953): 18-19.

45. Brou, "Études," 95.

46. *Historia persecutionis*, 3.3-14 (*CSEL* 7, 72-78).

47. Courtois, *Les Vandales*, 290-303.

48. Collects 23, 75, 119, 128, 147, and 150.

49. *The war of spiritual evil*, appears in collects 23, 75, 128, and 147.

50. See "Collect 150 as a Thematic Summary," on page 46.

51. Collect 75.

52. Collects 5, 34, and 75.

53. Collect 75.

54. Collects 10 and 37.

55. Fulgentius treats Psalm 37 as part of the Penitential Psalms in chapter 3.

56. Collects 2, 45, 62, 77, 80, 84, 93, 96, 114, 134, 135 and 150.

57. Collects 104, 109, and 118.4.

58. *Historia persecutionis*, 1.3-4 (*CSEL* 7, 1-2).

59. Societé Historique Algérienne, *Vingt-cinq ans d'histoire Algérienne: recherches et publications*, vol. 2 (Algiers: Gouvernment General de l'Algérie, 1950), 36.

60. Courtois, *Tablettes Albertini: actes privés de l'epoque Vandale* (Paris: Arts et Metiers Graphiques, 1952).

61. *Aquilo* appears in collect 106; *constituto* appears in collects 22 and 87; *coram* appears in collects 61 and 142.

62. Courtois, *Les Tablettes*, 202.

63. Collects 51 and 127.

64. Collects 4 and 22.

65. Collects 1, 66, 83, 84, 95, and 133.

66. Collect 4.

67. Collects 125.

68. Collect 4.

69. Collect 125.

70. Collect 4, with its reference to *the wine of apostolic doctrine*, connects to the feasting on wine at the table of wisdom from Prov. 9:1-6.

71. Collects 65, 66, 67, and 150.

72. Collect 82.

73. Collect 125.

74. Collects 56 and 91.

75. Collects 1, 83, 95, 118.21, and 133.

76. Collect 91.

77. Collects 79 and 131.

78. Collect 90.

79. *Seminat* is used in Matthew's and Luke's accounts (Mt. 13:1-51;

Lk. 8:5-15), and *seminus* is used by Mark (Mk. 4:3-32).

80. Jas. 5:7.

81. Collects 11, 71, 73, 81, and 131.

82. Collects 71 and 73, a thematic pocket.

83. Collect 38.

84. Collect 118.10.

85. Collect 118.17.

86. Mk. 10:21; Mt. 6:19-21; Lk. 18:22; Acts 3:6.

87. P. Verbracken, in *Oraisons sur les 150 psaumes* (Paris: Les Éditions du Cerf, 1967), 49 offers a translation that makes better theological sense of collect 14 than a more literal translation: . . . *fait de nous les habitants de tabernacle éternel. Ne tolère pas que nous acceptions jamais de présents pour perdre l'innocent, mais permets á notre misère de confier ton argent aux pauvres: ainsi, tu ne nous couronneras de tes propres bienfaits.*

88. Fulgentius usually employs the term *domus* in petitions that express the desire to dwell in the Lord's house in collects 22, 26, 51, 57, 91, 100, 117, 124, 133, and 147. He uses *atrium* in this sense in collects 4 and 121. Collect 4 contains the sole use of *tabernaculum*.

89. See n. 88 for Verbracken's French rendering.

90. Could these unusual petitions have the purpose of forming questions in the minds of the monks, to be answered at a later community meeting or in a homily?

91. 1Cor. 13:1.

Chapter 3

1. Origen's five homilies on Ps. 36 and two homilies on Pss. 37 and 38 have survived in Latin translation (*PG* 12, 1319-1410).

2. An explanation of Origen's interpretative method appears in H. Crouzel, *Origen*, trans. A. Worral (San Francisco: Harper and Row, 1989), 64-78, and in J. Trigg, *Origen* (Atlanta: John Knox Press, 1983), 230-232.

3. Hilary, *Tractatus super Psalmos* (PL 9, 231-908). Only commentaries on Pss. 1, 2, 9, 13, 14, 51-59, 91, and 118-150 survive.

Jerome recognizes Hilary's use of Origen's method in *De uiris illustribus*, 100 (*PL* 23, 699).

4. Hilary, *Tractatus super Psalmos*, Prologue (*PL* 9, 246-47.

5. Ambrose's homilies appear in *CSEL* 62 and 64. See also H. J. auf der Maur, *Das Psalmenverständnis des Ambrosius von Mailand* (Leiden: E. J. Brill, 1977) 243-301. Ambrose, like Fulgentius, treats

each stanza of Ps. 118 separately, giving one homily to each of the twenty-two.

6. Maur, *Das Psalmenverständnis*, 315-16. Collects 47, 71, 77, and 102 address David's prophetic character.

7. auf der Maur, *Das Psalmenverständnis*, 321-23.

8. *Confessiones*, 5.14.24 (*CSEL* 33, 111-112.). See also Trigg, *Origen*, 250-51.

9. S. Hebgin's introduction to *St. Augustine on the Psalms*, *ACW* 29 (Westminster MD: The Newman Press, 1960), 5-11; 17-19, treats Augustine's scholarly approach to the Psalms.

10. Brou, *Collects*, 23.

11. R. Holub, *Reception Theory*, 11.

12. E. Auerbach, *Literary Language and Its Public* (London: Routledge and Kegan Paul, 1965), 32.

13. Collects 12, 15, 30, 34, 47, 78, 95, 112, 117, 122 and 144 employ direct quotations from the psalms that they accompany. Collect 45 quotes directly from Ps. 119:1. In the translation of the collects in the Appendix, verses quoted verbatim appear in capitals, and words paraphrased closely from the psalm appear in italics.

14. The community's confidence is such that the "accusation" portion of the lament psalms do not receive interpretation in the collects.

15. H. Gunkel, *Einleitung in die Psalmen* (Götingen: Vandenhoek und Ruprecht, 1932). Most of the material used in this study can be found in the abridged translation: *The Psalms: A Form-Critical Introduction*, trans. T. Horner (Philadelphia: Fortress Press, 1946).

16. Pss. 116 and 150, the two briefest psalms, cannot help but to receive complete interpretations, and, in the case of Ps. 150, Fulgentius has composed a collect that approaches the status of commentary.

17. Gunkel, *The Psalms*, 11-12.

18. W. Brueggemann, *The Message of the Psalms* (Minneapolis: Augsburg Publishing House, 1984), 26.

19. 1Cor. 3:2.

20. Phil. 2:6-11.

21. Mt. 9:13; 12:7.

22. Lactantius and Augustine affirmed the existence of demons and their affect on people, which includes eliciting false worship. Two studies of this theme in these authors are: E. Schneweis, "Angels and Demons According to Lactantius" (PhD. Diss., Catholic University of America, 1944); E. van Antwerp, "Saint Augustine: The

Divination of Demons and the Care of the Dead" (Ph.D. Diss., Catholic University of America, 1955).

23. Rev. 20.

24. The phrase, *fruits of divine cultivation* and similar phrases also appear in collects 1, 95, and 133.

25. *Rule*, 2.3. Augustine requires attention of the heart to prayer; G. Lawless, *Augustine and His Monastic Rule* (Oxford: The Clarendon Press, 1987), 84-85.

26. Rom. 8-9; 1Cor. 3.

27. The term, *Opus Dei*, will appear as the title for monastic prayer in Benedict's *Rule*.

28. Fulgentius's employment of the themes of light and darkness echo those that appear in the *Didache* 1.1-6.1, trans. C. Richardson, *ECF* 1 (London: SCM Press, Ltd., 1953), 171-74; Pseudo-Barnabas 18-20, *Epître de Barnabé*, ed. R. S. Kraft (Paris: Les Éditions du Cerf, 1971), 194-214.

29. Pss. 5:8; 10:5; 78:1; 137:2, and Sir. 49:14; Jon. 2:5; 2:8; Mic. 1:2; Hab. 2:20; 2Macc. 9:16; 13:11; 14:31.

30. 1Cor. 3:16, 17; 6:19; 2Cor. 6:16; Eph. 2:21.

31. S. Mowinckel, trans. D. Ap-Thomas, *The Psalms in Israel's Worship* (Nashville: Abingdon, 1962), 2, 131. Mowinckel addresses the atypical elements in this description of humanity.

32. Heb. 2:5-8.

33. Rom. 3:21-31.

34. Collect 86 poses several editorial problems; see Brou, *Collects*, 92.

35. Collect 86 evokes *et homo factus est*, from the Nicene Creed.

36. A. Souter, *A Glossary of Later Latin*, 344.

37. R. Murphy, "Psalms," *JBC*, 1, 574.

38. Fulgentius does not interpret psalm titles.

39. Collects 19, 44, and 131.

40. Collects 2, 71. and 109.

41. Collects 2, 20, and 44.

42. Mk. 10:23-24; Mt. 19:23-24; Lk. 18:24-25.

43. Mowinckel, *The Psalms in Israel's Worship*, 66.

44. Modern speech act theory holds that the spoken word in some contexts performs the act that it signifies; J. Austin, *How to Do Things With Words* (Cambridge: Cambridge University Press, 1969).

45. Rom. 12; 1Cor. 6: 12; Eph. 3: 5: Col. 3.

46. 2Cor. 8; 9; Eph. 1; 2.

47. R. Gregg, *Early Arianism* (Philadelphia: Fortress Press, 1981),

60.

48. J. N. D. Kelly *Early Christian Doctrine*, rev. ed. (San Francisco: Harper and Row, 1979), 227.

49. Gunkel, in *Einleitung*, 384-387, used the term, *Weisheitdichtung*.

50. In Hebrew, *hwqmh*.

51. Brueggemann, *The Message of the Psalms*, 38-39.

52. Jn.15:1. The phrase, *the fruits of divine culture (fructus diuine culture)*, appears in collects 83 and 85. Collect 118.21 contains the phrase, *diuine culture*.

53. Pss. 77, 104, and 105 are historical psalms. Pss. 114, 134 and 135 are hymns of praise. Ps. 80 is an oracular liturgical psalm.

54. Collects 80, 104, and 113.

55. Collects 77, 104, and 134.

56. Collect 105.

57. Collects 19 and 135.

58. H. J. Krauss, *Theology of the Psalms* (Minneapolis: Augsburg Publishing House, 1979), 51.

59. Ex. 20:2; Dt. 5:6.

60. Collect 77 employs verses 4, 5, 7, 24, 16, 14, 13, 53, and 54, in listed order, from Ps. 77.

61. 1Cor. 10:4.

62. The theme of the living waters as employed in the collect appears in Jn. 4, especially, but also in Jn. 19:34;5; Rev. 7:17; 21:6.

63. Ex. 14:24-25.

64. Ex. 24: 40.

65. Num. 16.

66. Augustine, in his *Enarrationes in Psalmos* (*CC* 40), 1561, interprets the fate of Dathan and Abiram in a similar manner.

67. *Historia persecutionis* 1.22 (*CSEL* 7, 10-11).

68. Courcelle, *Histoire litteaire*, 36.

69. Ps. 19:7 reads: *I know that the Lord saved His Anointed; He will hear Him from His holy heaven in the powers of his saving right arm.*

70. Pss. 6, 31, 37, 50, 101, 129 and 142.

71. Gunkel, *Einleitung*, 131-32; 251-52.

72. Possidius, *Vita Augustini*, 31 (*PL* 32, 63).

73. Dr. Harry Nasuti, of Fordham University, is researching the Augustinian connection to the Penitential Psalms. I am grateful to him for letting me see some of his research prior to its publication.

74. Cassiodorus, *Expositio psalmorum* (*PL* 70).

75. Pss. 6, 101, and 142.

76. Forms of *peccatum* appear in 23 collects other than 6, 31 and 142; forms of *iniquitas* appear in 9 collects other than 129; a form of *mortificatum* appears in collect 33 as well as 142. *Infirmitas* appears in collect 6 only and *iniusticia nostra* appears in collect 101 only.

77. Ps. 50:4, *wash me from my iniquities.*

78. Ps. 50:5, *I know my iniquity.*

79. *He freed the offspring of the dead.*

80. The phrase *mortificatorum filios* also appears in collect 78, which states, *receive in adoption the offspring of the dead.*

81. The other penitential collects display less emotion than collect 37 when dealing with God's wrath. Collects 31 and 129 simply request deliverance.

The petitions of collects 50 and 142, which ask that God not cast off or judge repentant sinners, follow acknowledgement of sin.

82. Ps. 37:1-3, *Lord, in your rage do not accuse me, nor in your anger rebuke me, for your arrows are fixed in me.*

83. Ps. 101:4, *my days vanished like smoke.*

84. Ps. 6:3 asks for healing of the psalmist's bones, and its collect asks healing for the community's souls. Ps. 37:4 declares that the psalmist has health neither in flesh nor bones. Its collect asks for God to *heal our bones.*

85. Collects 34, 43, 48, 68, and 118.18 ask for redemption. Penitential collect 31 asks for redemption from unnamed pressures. Penitential collect 129 broadens the view of those needing redemption, characterizing them as *Israel.*

86. Collect 129 employs the verb *parco* (forgive), which appears also in collects 35, 136, 137, and 149 as well.

Collects 35 and 136 use the verb in a chain of petitions with no stated object. Collect 137 asks for forgiveness of sins. As a portion of collect 149 is lost, its use of *parco* remains unclear.

87. Gunkel, *The Psalms: Structure, Content and Message* (Minneapolis: Augsburg Publishing House, 1980), 14, 32; Westermann, *The Psalms*, 59.

Collect 101 also expresses confidence, but gives a more specific reason for the confidence, *you have already looked favorably upon the adoration of the humble.*

88. *Do not enter into judgment with your servant, for no living person is justified in your sight.*

Chapter 4

1. Brou, *Collects*, 24.
2. Chapter 3 contains a discussion of Fulgentius's literary background.
3. Discussed in chapter 3.
4. Vigilius wrote in the last quarter of the fifth century. His *Aduersus Eutychtetem* (*PL* 62, 1157-1172) deals with the Three Chapters controversy.
5. Liberatus was active in the middle of the sixth century. His *Breuiarum causae Nestorianorum et Eutychianorum* (*PL* 63, 969) challenges the christology of Eutyches.
6. The writings and person of Theodore of Mopsuestia, a teacher of Nestorius, were condemned, as well as some writings of Theodoret of Cyrus and Ibas of Eddesa.
7. Pontianus brings his dissent to the emperor himself in *Epistola de tribus capitulis ad Iustiniam Imperatorum* (*PL* 68, 995-998).
8. Chapter 1 contains an overview of the writings of Facundus and Verecundus.
9. Collects 1, 4, 6, 10, 15, 18, 48, 52, 60, 74, 77, 80, 81, 96, 98, 99, 107, 114, 118.5, 118.13, 118.16, 120, 121, and 142.
10. Collects 10, 14, 113, 118.4, and 118.18.
11. Collects 21, 24, 28, 35, 46, 47, 51, 58, 60, 73, 76, 78, 85, 88, 98, 122, 140, 141, and 146.
12. Collects 10, 15, 18, 52, 60, 77, 80, 96, 98, 99, 118.5, 118.7, 118.10, 120, 122, 140, 141, and 146.
13. Collects 1, 6, 114, 121, and 142.
14. Collects 10, 14, 15, 58, 80, 96, 113, 118.4, 118.16, 118.18, and 141.
15. Collects 4 and 111.
16. For an overview of Augustine's thought on grace, see J. P. Burns, *The Development of Augustine's Doctrine of Operative Grace* (Paris: Études augustiniennes, 1980), 18-21.
17. Burns, *The Development*, 31.
18. G. Nygren, "The Augustinian Conception of Grace," *SP* 2, 1957: 258-269.
19. V. Campanaga, "La doctrina Agustiana de la gracia en los Salmos," *SP* 6, 1962: 334-336.
20. The middle of collect 96 is a poetic evocation of the power of the Holy Spirit.
21. Augustine's *Expositio quarumdam propositionum ex epistola ad*

Romanos, 13-18, trans. and ed. P. Landres in *Augustine on Romans* (Chico, CA: The Scholar's Press, 1982), 4-7. The four stages of the life in grace are: *ante legem, sub Lege, sub gratia, in pace.*

22. Rom. 6:6-11; Eph. 4:22-24; Col. 3:9-10.

23. H. Rondet, "La théologie de la grâce dans la correspondance de saint Augustin," *Recherches augustiniennes* 1 (1958): 305; also, Burns, *The Development*, 34-35.

24. Rondet, "La Théologie," 304.

25. 1Tim. 2:5.

26. Interestingly, the name "Meribah" does not appear in the two Latin versions in the Stuttgart edition (Pss. 80, 94, and 105). Both the translation from the Septuagint and from Hebrew use the term *aquas contradictionis*.

Fulgentius's mention of temptation recalls a similar petition from the Lord's Prayer (Mt. 6:13), as well as 2Thess. 3:3 and Jas. 1:13.

27. Augustine, *Enarrationes in Psalmos* 80, 8-10 (*CSEL* 39, 1124-25). interprets the *waters* of verse 8 in terms of baptism. The collects refrain from invoking sacramental theology, but Fulgentius's use of the term *aquas contradictionis* indicates that he did not interpret the verse soteriologically, while Augustine clearly sees that, now that the four stages of salvation are available to people, they turn the waters of contradiction into the saving grace of Christian baptism.

28. Acts 26:18 and Col. 1:13.

29. Collect 78 treats Exodus themes in the light of grace similarly to collects 113 and 114.

30. Fulgentius employs various terms to indicate sin and sinfulness: *infirmitas*, in collect 6; *peccatum* in collects 3, 6, 7, 17, 27, 31, 38, 40, 54, 59, 61, 73, 74, 78, 102, 118.5, 118.6, 118.8, 115.15, 118.19, 123, 139, 142, 145, and 150; *inlusio* in collect 37; *iniustitia* in collect 50; *mortificatio*, in collects 78 and 101; *iniquitas* in collects 7, 27, 28, 48, 56, 63, 84, 118.18, 129, and 140; *malum* in collects 33 and 142. Collect 18 refers to *nostra oculta*, indicating secret faults.

31. Burns, *The Development*, 19.

32. *Expositio quarumdum propositionum*, 13-18, trans. and ed. Landes, 4-7.

33. See collect 35 for an expression of Body of Christ theology.

34. Burns, *The Development*, 34.

35. "Groan" (*gemitus*) appears in collects 11, 47, 78, and 101. "Tear" (*lacrima*) appears in collects 55, 79, 114 and 125.

36. Rom. 8:18.

37. Collect 118.20, *May our eyes hasten to meditate upon your*

words.

38. *RB* 5.14; 34.6; 40.8-9.

39. Burns, *The Development*, 22.

40. Fulgentius treats the symbol of light often in the collects. Collects 12, 17, 26, 35, 88, 118.19, and 139 take the theme from their psalm texts. In his sermon on psalm 66, which contains light imagery that Fulgentius does not exploit in its collect, Augustine compares light to God's wisdom, capable of enlightening an individual with the divine image, in *Enarrationes in Psalmos* 66.4 (*CC* 39, 861). See also, Campanaga, "La doctrina," 340-42.

41. Lk. 12:15-21.

42. Campanaga, "La doctrina," 343. See also Augustine, *De Trinitate*, 4.2.4 (*PL* 42, 899).

43. Mt. 20:20;28; Mk. 10:35-45; Lk. 22:24-27.

44. *Ep.* 194 (*CSEL* 57, 176-214).

45. *Ep.* 214 (*CSEL* 57, 387-96). See also B. Rees, *Pelagius: A Reluctant Heretic* (Wolfeboro, NH: The Boydell Press, 1988), 101-103.

46. For the translation of christological terms from Greek to Latin, see R. Braun, *"Deus Christianorum": Recherches sur le vocabulaire doctrinal de Tertullian* (Paris: Presses Universitaires de France, 1962).

Verbum is one of Tertullian's two translations for the Greek *logos*. The other term, *sermo*, does not appear in the collects.

47. A. Grillmeier, trans. J. Bowden, *Christ in Christian Tradition* (Atlanta: John Knox Press, 1975), 1: 447.

48. *Ep.* 4 (*PG* 77, 43-50).

49. Grillmeier, *Christ in Christian Tradition*, 1: 545.

50. J. Morgan, *The Importance of Tertullian in the Development of Christian Dogma* (London: Kegan Paul, Trench, Trubner and Co., 1928), 32, 90.

51. See Leo I's *Ep.* 28.3, the *Tomus ad Flavianum*, (*PL* 54, 763).

52. Eph. 4:24 and Col. 3:9-10.

53. Ps. 67:5.

54. Collects 18, 118.12 and 118.22 use the term, *uerbum*, but the christological connection, if any, is unclear.

55. Gen. 36:8.

Conclusion

1. Collects 42, 91, 107, 116, 130, 131, 135, and 142.

SOURCES

Liturgical, Scriptural and Concilliar Sources

Gallican Psalter, or *Psalter of Charlemagne.* La Salle des Manuscrits, La Bibliothèque National, Paris (B. N. lat. 13159).

Gallican Psalter, or *Psalter of Charlemagne.* Bodleian Library, Oxford (MS Douce, 59).

The Psalter Collects from V-VIth Century Sources, ed. Louis Brou. London: Harrison and Sons, Ltd., 1949.

Sacrorum conciliorum noua et amplissima collectio, ed. Giovanno Mansi. Florence-Venice, 1759-98.

Vindicae canonicorum Scriptorum Vulgatae Latinae editionis, ed. Giovanni Bianchini. Rome, 1740.

Patristic Sources

Aetheria, *Itinerarium.CSEL* 24.

Augustine. *Confessiones. CC* 27.

————. *De baptismo. CSEL* 51.

————. *Enarrationes in Psalmos. CC* 38-40.

————. *De gratia et libero arbitrio. PL* 44.

Cassian, John. *Institutiones coenobiorum. CSEL* 17.

Didache, trans. C. Richardson. London: SCM Press, Ltd., 1953.

Facundus of Hermiane. *Epistola fidei catholicae in defensione trium capitulorum. PL* 67.

_____. *Pro defensione trium capitulorum. PL* 67.

Ferrandus, Deacon of Carthage. *Breuiatio canonum. PL* 67.

_____. *Epistolae* 3, 5. *PL* 67.

_____. *Vita s. Fulgentii*, ed. G. Lapeyre. Paris: Lethielleux, 1929.

Fulgentius of Ruspe. *Ad Euthymium de remissione peccatorum. CC* 91.

_____. *Ad Monimum. CC* 91.

_____. *Ad Thrasamundum regem Vandalorum. CC* 91.

_____. *Contra Arianos. PL* 65.

_____. *Contra sermonem Fastidiosi Ariani, ad Victorem. CC* 91.

_____. *De ueritate praedestinationis. CC* 91A.

_____. *Dicta regis Thrasamundi et contra ea responsionum. CC* 91.

_____. *Epistolae* 7, 14. *CC*. 91.

_____. *Epistola* 17. *CC* 91A.

_____. *Pro fide catholica, aduersus Pintam episcopum Arianum. PL* 65.

_____. *Sermones* 1, 2. *CC* 91A.

_____. *Sermo* 78. *PL* 65.

Hilary of Poitiers. *Tractatus super Psalmos. PL* 9.

Jerome. *De uiris illustribus. PL* 23.

Leo I. *Epistola 28* (*Tomus ad Flavianum*). *PL* 54.

Optatus. *Sermo in natali Sanctorum Innocentium. PLS*, 1.

Origen. *Homiliae super Psalmos* 36, 37, 38, trans. Rufinus. *PG* 12.

Passio septem monachorum. CSEL 7.

Pontianus of Ignota. *Epistola de tribus capitulis ad Iustinian Imperatorem. PL* 68.

Possidius. *Vita Augustini. PL* 50.

Procopius of Caesarea. *De bello vandalico*, trans. H. B. Dewing. Cambridge, MA: Harvard University Press, 1953.

Pseudo-Athanasius. *De uirginitate siue Ascesi. PG* 28.

Pseudo-Barnabas. *Epître de Barnabé*, ed. R. S. Kraft. Paris: Les Éditions du Cerf, 1971.

Regula Magistri, trans. and ed. A. de Vogüe. Paris: Les Éditions du Cerf, 1964.

Tertullian. *Apologeticus. CSEL* 69.

Verecundus of Junca. *Commentarium super cantica ecclestica. CC* 93.

_____. *Crisias. SS.*

_____. *Excerptiones de gestis Chalcedonensis concilii. SS.*

_____. *Exhortatio Poenitendi. SS.*

Victor of Vita. *Historia persecutionis Africanae provinciae. CSEL* 8.

Literature

Auerbach, Erich. *Literary Language and Its Public in Late Latin Antiquity and in the Middle Ages*. London: Routledge and Kegan Paul, 1965.

Auf der Maur, H. J. *Das Psalmenverständnis des Ambrosius von Mailand*. Leiden: E. J. Brill, 1977.

Austin, John. *How to Do Things With Words*. Cambridge, MA: Harvard University Press, 1962.

Battifol, P. *A History of the Roman Breviary*, trans. A. Baylay. New York: Longmans, Green and Co., 1912.

Ben Adeb, Aicha. *Carthage: A Mosaic of Ancient Tunisia*. New York: W. W. Norton and Company, 1987.

Boucher, Edmund. *Life and Letters in Roman Africa*. Oxford: Blackwell, 1913.

Bradshaw, Paul. *Daily Prayer in the Early Church: A Study of the Origin and Development of the Divine Office*. New York: Oxford University Press, 1982.

Bright, David. *The Miniature Epic in Vandal North Africa*. Norman, OK: The University of Oklahoma Press, 1987.

Brou, Louis. "Ou en la question des 'Psalter Collects'?" *SP* 2 (1957): 12-20.

_____. "Etudes sur les collectes du psautier: 1 La série africaine et l'Evêque Verecundus de Junca." *Sacris Erudiri* 6 (1954):73-95.

Brown, Peter. "Christianity and Local Culture in Late Roman North Africa." *JRS* 58 (1968):83-96.

Brueggeman, Walter. *The Message of the Psalms*. Minneapolis: Augsburg Publishing House, 1984.

_____. *Israel's Praise: Doxology Against Idolatry and Ideology.* Philadelphia: The Fortress Press, 1988.

Burns, J. *The Development of Augustine's Doctrine of Operative Grace.* Paris: Etudes augustiniennes, 1980.

Campanaga, Victorino. "La doctrina Augustiana de la gracia en los Salmos." *SP* 6 (1962): 315-349.

Capelle, Paul. *Le Texte du psautier latin en Afrique.* Rome: F. Pustet, 1913.

_____. "Actualité des ancien psautiers latins." *Revue d'histoire ecclésiastique* 55 (1960), 492-498.

Chadwick, Henry. *Augustine.* Oxford: Oxford university Press, 1986.

Chirat, Henri, Review of *The Psalter* Collects From V-VI Century Sources, by Louis Brou. In *Revue du Moyen Age Latin* 5 (1949), 247-254.

Childs, B. "Psalm Titles and Midrashic Exegesis." *JSS*, 16 (1971): 137-150.

Clark, M. C. *Rhetoric at Rome.* London: Cohen and West, Ltd., 1953.

Cochrane, Charles. *Christianity and Classical Culture.* Oxford: Oxford University Press, 1940.

Courcelle, P. *Histoire littéraire des grandes invasions germaniques.* Paris: Etudes augustiniennes, 1964.

Courtois, Christian. *Tablettes Albertini: actes privés de l'epoque Vandale.* Paris: Arts et Metiers Graphiques, 1952.

_____. *Les Vandales et l'Afrique.* Paris: Arts et Metiers Graphiques, 1955.

Crouzel, Henri. *Origen,* trans. A. Worrall. San Francisco: Harper and Row, 1989.

Decarraux, O. *Monks and Civilization: From the Barbarian Invasions to the Reign of Charlemagne*, trans. C. Haldane. Garden City, NY: Doubleday and Co., 1964.

Diesner, H. J. *Fulgentius von Ruspe als Theologe und Kirchenpolitiker.* Stuttgart: Calwer Verlag, 1966.

_____. "Fulgentius von Ruspe und einige Probleme der vandalenzeitlichen Patristik in Nordafrika." *SP* 10/1 (1970), 285-290.

_____. *The Great Migration: The Movement of Peoples Across Europe, A.D. 300-700.* London: Orbis Pub. Co., 1978.

_____. *Kirche un Staat im spätrömischen Reich.* Berlin: Evangelische Verlaganstalt, 1963.

Duckett, Eleanor. *Latin Writers of the Fifth Century.* New York: Holt and Co., 1930.

Dugmore, Clifford. *The Influence of the Synagogue on the Divine Office.* Westminster: The Faith Press, Ltd., 1944.

Finkel, Asher. "Yabneh's Liturgy and Early Christianity." *JES* 18 (1981): 231-250.

Fischer, Bonifatius. *Novae Concordantiae Bibliorum Sacrorum iuxta Vulgata Versionem criticie editam.* Stuttgart: Friedrich Fromman Verlag, 1977.

Frend, W. H. C. *The Donatist Church: A Movement of Protest in Roman North Africa.* Oxford: The Clarendon Press, 1952.

_____. "The Gnostic-Manichaean Tradition in Roman North Africa." *JEH* 4 (1953): 13-26.

Gavigan, John. *De vita monastica in Africa septentrionali inde a temporibus S. Augustini usque ad invasiones Arabum.* Rome: Marietti, 1962.

Gibbon, Edward, ed. J. Bury. *The Decline and Fall of the Roman*

Empire. New York: The Heritage Press, 1962.

Gregg, R. *Early Arianism: A View of Salvation*. Philadelphia: Fortress Press, 1981.

Grillmeier, Aloys. *Christ in Christian Tradition. Volume 1: From the Apostolic Age to Chalcedon (451)*, trans. J. Bowden. Atlanta: John Knox Press, 1975.

Guilding, A. "Some Obscured Rubrics and Lectionary Allusions in the Psalter." *JTS*, 35 (1934): 41-55.

Gunkel, Hermann. *Einleitung in die Psalmen: Die Gattungen der religiösen Lyrik Israels*. Göttingen: Vandenhoek und Ruprecht, 1933.

_____. *The Psalms: A Form-Critical Introduction*, trans. T. Horner. Philadelphia: The Fortress Press, 1967.

Hebgin, S. *St. Augustine on the Psalms*. Westminster, MD: The Newman Press, 1960.

Heiming, Odilo. "Zum monastischen Offizium von Kassianus bis Kolumbanus." *Archiv für Liturgiwissenschaft* 7 (1961): 89-156.

Holub, Robert. *Reception Theory: A Critical Introduction*. London: Methuen, 1984.

Jauss, Hans. *Towards and Aesthetic of Reception*, trans. T. Bahti. Minneapolis, MN: University of Minnesota Press, 1982.

_____. *Aesthetic Experience and Literary Hermeneutics*, trans. M. Shaw. Minneapolis, MN: University of Minnesota Press, 1982.

Jones, A. H. M. "Were Ancient Heresies National or Social Movements in Disguise?" *JTS* 10 (1959): 281-289.

Julien, Ch. *Histoire de l'Afrique du Nord*. Paris: Payot, 1951.

Jungmann, Josef. *The Early Liturgy to the Time of Gregory the Great*, trans. F. Brunner. Notre Dame, IN: University of Notre Dame Press, 1959.

_____. *Pastoral Liturgy*. New York: Herder and Herder, 1962.

Kelly, J. N. D. *Early Christian Doctrines*, rev. ed. San Francisco: Harper and Row, 1979.

Kennedy, George. *The Art of Rhetoric in the Roman World*. Princeton: Princeton University Press, 1972.

_____. *Classical Rhetoric and Its Christian and Secular Tradition from Ancient to Modern Times*. Chapel Hill, NC: The University of North Carolina Press, 1980.

_____. *Power and Persuasion in Late Antuiquity: Towards a Christian Empire*. Madison, WI: The University of Wisconsin Press, 1992.

Kozelka, Leo. *Das leben des hl. Fulgentius von Diakon Ferrandus von Kathargo*. Munich: Verlag Josef Kösel and Friedrich Pustet, 1934.

Kraus, Hans. *Theology of the Psalms*. Minneapolis: Augsburg Publishing House, 1979.

Labriolle, Pierre. *History and Literature of Christianity: From Tertullian to Boethius*, trans. H. Wilson. New York: Knopf, 1925.

Lawless, G. *Saint Augustine and His Monastic Rule*. Oxford: The Clarendon Press, 1987.

Leclerc, H. *L'Afrique chrétienne*, 2 vols. Paris: Librairie Lecoffre, 1904.

Leclerq, J. "Les inédits africains de l'homilaire de Fleury." *Revue bénédictine* 58 (1948): 53-72.

_____. "Anciennes prières monastiques." *Studia monastica* 1

(1959): 379-392.

Leroquais, C. *Les Psautiers manuscrits latins des bibliothèques publiques de france.* Macon: Protat Frères, 1940.

Linton, O. "Interpretation of Psalms in the Early Church." *SP* 4 (1959): 143-156.

Lowe, E. A. *Codices latini antiquiores: A Paleographical Guide to Latin Manuscripts Prior to the Ninth Century,* Vol. 5. Oxford: Clarendon Press, 1950.

MacKendrick, Paul. *The North African Stones Speak.* Chapel Hill, NC: The University of North Carolina Press, 1980.

MacMullen, Ramsey. *Enemies of the Roman Order.* Cambridge, MA: Harvard University Press, 1966.

_____. "Provincial Languages in the Roman Empire." *AJP* 87 (1966): 1-14.

_____. "A Note on *Sermo Humilis*." *JTS* 17 (1966): 108-112.

_____. *Christianizing the Roman Empire (A. D. 100-400).* New Haven: Yale University Press, 1984.

Markus, Robert. *The End of Ancient Christianity.* Cambridge: Cambridge University Press, 1990.

Martroye, François. *L'occident à l'èpoque byzantine: Goths et Vandales.* Paris: Librairie Hachette, 1904.

Mateos, J. "L'Office monastique à la fin du IVe siècle." *Oriens Christianus* 47 (1963): 53-88.

_____. "Quelques anciens documents sur l'Office du soir." *Orientalia Christiana* 35 (1969): 347-374.

Mohrmann, Christine. "A Propos des Collectes du Psautier." *VC* 6 (1952): 1-19.

Monceaux, Paul. *Histoire littéraire de l'Afrique chrétienne depuis les origines jusqu'à l'invasion arabe*, 7 vols. Brussels: Ed. Culture et Civlisation, 1963.

Morgan, J. *The Importance of Tertullian in the Development of Christian Dogma*. London: Kegan Paul, Trench, Trubner and Co., 1928.

Mowinckel, Sigmund, trans. D. Ap-Thomas. *The Psalms in Israel's Worship*. Nashville: Abingdon, 1962.

Musset, L. *The Germanic Invasions: The Making of Europe A. D. 400-600*. London: Paul Elek, 1975.

National Conference of Catholic Bishops. *Christian Prayer: The Liturgy of the Hours*. New York: Catholic Book Publishing Co., Inc., 1976.

Nygren, G. "The Augustinian Conception of Grace." *SP* 2 (1957): 258-269.

Palanque, J. *Le christianisme et l'occident barbare*. Stuttgart: Calwer Verlag, 1966.

Pfaff, Richard. "Psalter Collects as an Aid to the Classification of Psalters." *SP* 18, 2 (1989): 397-402.

Randers-Pehrson, Justine. *Barbarians and Romans: The Birth Struggle of Europe, A. D. 400-700*. London: Croom Helm, 1983.

Rees, Bryn. *Pelagius: A Reluctant Heretic*. Wolfeboro, NH: The Boydell Press, 1988.

Rondet, Henri. "La théologie de la grace dans la correspondance de saint Augustin." *Recherches augustiniennes* 1 (1958), 303-315.

Salmon, Pierre. "Richesses et deficiences des anciens psautiers latins." *Collectanea Biblica Latina* 13. Rome: Abbey of Saint Jerome, 1959.

Sawyer, J. "An Analysis of the Content and Meaning of the Psalm Headings." *Transactions of the Glasgow University Oriental Society*, 22 (1967-68): 26-38.

Schamoni, Wilhelm. *Bischöfe der alten afrikanischen Kirche*. Düsseldorf: Patmos, 1964.

Schneweis, Emil. "Angels and Demons According to Lactantius." Ph.D. diss., Catholic University of America, 1944.

Searle, John. *Speech Acts: An Essay on the Philosophy of Language*. Cambridge: Cambridge University Press, 1969.

Simpson, R. *The Interpretation of Prayer in the Early Church*. Philadelphia: The Westminster Press, 1965.

Slomovic, E. "Toward an Understanding of the Formation of Historical Titles in the Book of Psalms." *ZAW*, 91 (1979): 350-380.

Smalley, Beryl, ed. *Trends in Medieval Political Thought*. New York: Barnes and Noble, 1965.

Societé Historique Algérienne. *Vingt-cing ans d'histoire Algérienne: recherches et publications*. Algiers: Gouvernment Général de l'Algérie, 1950.

Souter, Alexander. *A Glossary of Later Latin to 600 A. D.* Oxford: The Clarendon Press, 1949.

Stevens, Susan. "The Circle of Bishop Fulgentius." *Traditio* 38 (1982), 327-341.

Strelka, J. *Theories of Literary Genre*. University Park, PA: Pennsylvania State University Press, 1978.

Taft, Robert. *The Liturgy of the Hours in the East and West: The Origins of the Divine Office and Its Meaning for Today*. Collegeville: The Liturgical Press, 1986.

Thesaurus Augustinianus. Turnholt: Brepols. 1989, text-fiche.

GENERAL INDEX

SCRIPTURAL INDEX